Is Your Pet Psychic?

Developing Psychic Communication with Your Pet

Richard Webster

2002
Llewellyn Publications
St. Paul, Minnesota 55164-0383, U.S.A.

FIRST EDITION
Second Printing, 2002

Book design and editing by Rebecca Zins
Cover design by Lisa Novak
Cover photographs © Photodisc

Library of Congress Cataloging-in-Publication Data

Webster, Richard.
    Is your pet psychic : developing psychic communication with your
    pet / Richard Webster.—1st ed.
        p.   cm.
    Includes bibliographical references (p.).
    ISBN 0-7387-0193-9
    1. Pets—Psychic aspects. 2. Extrasensory perception in animals. I. Title

SF412.5 .W425 2002
133.8'9—dc21   2001057999

Llewellyn Publications
A Division of Llewellyn Worldwide, Ltd.
P.O. Box 64383, Dept. 0-7387-0193-9
St. Paul, MN 55164-0383, U.S.A.
www.llewellyn.com

Printed in the United States of America

Listen to What Your Pet Has to Say

You probably know about some of the amazing feats regularly accomplished by animals, from salmon who navigate through hundreds of miles of water to their birthplace to spawn, to bloodhounds who can track the tiniest trace of a scent with noses one million times stronger than ours!

Although psychic powers such as telepathic communication have yet to be explained by modern science, all animals, both human and nonhuman, have the potential. But like any talent, psychic talent must be developed and practiced.

No matter what species your pet is—cat, dog, horse, or hamster—you can establish a psychic connection with him or her. Do you ever wish you and your pet could have a conversation? Next time you're alone together, try this experiment:

> *The most important part of hearing what your pet has to say is to simply remain receptive. Whenever you are stroking or cuddling your pet, think about the love you share and remain alert to any thoughts that pop into your mind. These may come as clear pictures, or simply as ideas. The response might even be a feeling in your heart, rather than a picture in your mind. Frequently you may not realize that the response has come from your pet, while at other times the thought could not have come from any other source. Remain impartial and accepting as the thoughts come in.*

About the Author

Richard Webster was born in New Zealand in 1946, and most of his earliest memories relate to animals of various sorts. As he grew up, he had a constant succession of pets, including dogs, cats, goats, rabbits, mice, turtles, tortoises, lizards, frogs, and fish. Currently, Richard and his wife have just two cats, a rabbit, and three fish. They also have three children and three grandchildren, all of whom share Richard's love of animals.

Richard has written many books, mainly on psychic subjects, and also writes monthly magazine columns. He would write more, but his pets tell him when it is time to stop and play.

Many of Llewellyn's authors have websites with additional information and resources. For more information, please visit our website at:

http://www.llewellyn.com

Other Books by Richard Webster

Astral Travel for Beginners

Aura Reading for Beginners

Dowsing for Beginners

Feng Shui for Beginners

Llewellyn Feng Shui series

Soul Mates

Spirit Guides and Angel Guardians

Numerology Magic

Omens, Oghams & Oracles

101 Feng Shui Tips for the Home

Palm Reading for Beginners

Seven Secrets for Success

Success Secrets: Letters to Matthew

Practical Guide to Past-Life Memories

Write Your Own Magic

Pendulum Magic

For my good friend
Ken Ring

Contents

Introduction . . . ix

1: The Amazing Natural Talents of Animals . . . 1

2: The Mysterious Cat . . . 15

3: Man's Best Friend . . . 35

4: The Noble Horse . . . 67

5: Animals Tall and Small . . . 87

6: Communicating with Your Pet . . . 93

7: Ghost Animals . . . 119

8: Pets Who Find Their Way Home . . . 141

9: Your Psychic Self . . . 155

10: Communicating with Your Pet in Dreams . . . 169

A New World . . . 181

Notes . . . 183

Suggested Reading . . . 201

Index . . . 209

INTRODUCTION

Animal lovers have always known the beneficial effects of owning a pet. However, it was not until 1975 that two English researchers, R. A. Mugford and J. G. M'Comisky, put it to the test. They gave caged birds to twelve pensioners, and gave another twelve a potted plant. Three months later, they found that the pensioners who had been given a bird both had a more positive outlook on life and a better attitude toward others than the pensioners who had been given a plant. Five years later, a study of people with heart disease found that pet owners were much more likely to be alive one year later than patients without a pet.[1] The research showed that ownership of a pet was the strongest single factor. It made no difference if the person was rich or poor, married or single, surrounded by friends or entirely alone. This confirms the belief of the Native Americans that without animals "men would die from great loneliness of spirit, for whatever happens to the beast also happens to man . . ."[2]

Pets often serve as psychologists and counselors for their human owners. By listening empathically, and responding to their owners' body language and thoughts, they surround their humans with a healing energy that takes away pain and hurt. This is even more powerful when the owners stroke and coddle their pets while talking to them.

There are more than two thousand programs in the United States where volunteers bring their pets to hospitals, retirement homes, and hospices to cheer and comfort the people there. These animals are frequently known as PAT ("pets as therapy") animals. I have also heard of similar programs in some prisons. The inmates who receive animal visitors are less aggressive and less likely to take drugs or commit suicide.[3]

Pet owners are often accused of being fanatical about their pets. A British survey appears to confirm this, as it found that 64 percent of pet owners would rather cuddle their pet than their partner. Another survey found that 50 percent of pet owners considered their pets to be better looking than their partners.[4]

In the early 1980s, it was estimated that forty million households in the United States contained dogs and twenty-three million homes contained cats.[5] If this figure is correct, it means that there is one dog for every six human beings. Dr. Stanley Coren, a professor of psychology at the University of British Columbia and author of several books on dogs, believes that there is one dog for every four families in North America.[6] In 1994, Dr. Bruce Fogle estimated that 38 percent of the homes in the United States contained at least one dog, and 30 percent of all homes contained at least one cat.[7] In 1998, it was estimated that there were 70 million cats and 57 million dogs in the United States. Thirty-four percent of the population owned at least one cat, and 37.8 percent owned at least one dog; 15.9 percent owned at least one cat and one dog.[8]

My mother frequently told me that only nice people have pets. I am sure there must be plenty of wonderful people in the world who do not have a pet, but by and large, I agree with my mother's comments. Pet owners are special people who enjoy a close, loving relationship with their animal friends. It is not surprising to me that many of them are in regular intuitive communication with their pets.

People decide to own pets for many reasons, usually for companionship or protection. No matter what the initial reason was, they soon find themselves inside an incredibly close and special relationship. Many people live rewarding lives solely because of the love they share with their pets. The healing effects that animals have on their owners are well-known.

Invariably, pet owners discover that their pet has abilities far beyond what they anticipated. Consequently, it is not surprising that sooner or later most animal-lovers wonder if their pet is psychic. Sometimes it is hard to know if an animal's behavior has a normal or paranormal explanation.

My daughter Charlotte works for a television station and has irregular hours. However, we always know when she is due home because her cat, Clyde, sits down at the front door ten minutes before she arrives. Over the years, people have come up with a variety of explanations for this not-uncommon behavior. Maybe Clyde senses that she is due home by picking up reactions from people in the house. This is not likely, as usually we have no idea when she will be arriving. Maybe Clyde hears her car coming. It would be surprising if he could hear her car when it was still ten minutes from home, but it is possible. However, this possibility was refuted the day Charlotte bought a new car. Ten minutes before she arrived home to show us her new car, Clyde was sitting in his usual spot waiting for her. I am certain there is a special telepathic bond between Clyde and Charlotte, and this enables him to know intuitively when she is due.

Alexandre Dumas (1802–1870), the famous author, had a cat that also knew when he was due home. When he was a young man, Dumas worked for the Duc d'Orleans. The office was a thirty-minute walk from Dumas' home. Every morning, his cat, Mysouff, would walk part of the way there with him. In the afternoon Mysouff would take himself back to the spot where the two had parted company and wait for his master's return. However, on the days when Dumas was unexpectedly delayed, Mysouff remained peacefully sleeping on his cushion. On every other day, Mysouff would scratch at the door until Dumas' mother let him out. As a result, Madam Dumas called Mysouff "her barometer," as she always knew when her son was delayed.[9]

Even more remarkable was Jim, a dog owned by Richard St. Barbe Baker. Each time he left the house, Jim would see him off, and would be waiting to welcome him home again on his return. Sometimes, though, Richard would come back by a different route that brought him through the big front gates at the entrance to the lodge. It did not matter whether he returned by the front or back gates. Jim always knew, and would be waiting at the correct entrance for him.[10]

When I was a child, early one morning, my father accidentally ran over and killed our cat. He buried him near an apple tree in our garden, and then carried on to work. None of us knew that our cat was dead until he returned home that evening. However, our Labrador dog knew. He lay on our cat's grave all day, and for the rest of his life lay on the site for several hours every day.

A friend of mine related a similar story involving a cat and a pet rabbit. When the rabbit died, the cat regularly sat on her friend's grave. These experiences are common. Virtually every time I relate one of these stories, someone will tell me of a similar experience that happened to one of their pets.

A short while ago, a couple told me of their pet cat Adolphe, a beautiful long-haired Siamese. He had a wonderful pedigree and his owners began exhibiting him at cat shows. Adolphe loved riding in the car, but hated the long days at the shows. The family gradually discovered this, as Adolphe would disappear shortly before they began getting ready to go to the show. They even tried locking him indoors the night before a show was to take place. This did not work either. As soon as his mistress opened the door to his room the next morning, he would run past her and disappear in the garden. He did not return until it was far too late to get to the show. Once the family realized how unhappy the shows made him, they stopped exhibiting him. Two years passed, and then the cat breeder who had sold Adolphe to them asked if they would exhibit him just one time at a special show in which she was going to receive an award. The family agreed, but on the morning of the show Adolphe was nowhere to be found. Although they were embarrassed at not being able to attend the show, they were not surprised, and have no intentions of ever trying to exhibit him again.

Naturally, not every experience can be termed psychic. We used to have a Labrador dog named Bruce who took himself to the veterinarian whenever he felt ill. The vet would treat him and then call us to pick him up. Everyone found this behavior amusing and appealing, but it is unlikely to be psychic. Bruce had learned from past experience that the vet could make him feel better. Consequently, if he felt unwell it made good sense to walk a couple of miles to see the person who could take the pain away.

Just about everyone has been brought up with talking animals. Popular movies, cartoons, children's books and comics all contain animals who not only talk to other members of the same species, but can usually also communicate with people. This is not a new phenomenon.

The folktales from almost every country also contain animals who talk to people.

Of course, children quickly learn that animals cannot talk to us in the way they do in the movies. They realize, though, that animals can and do communicate with us all the time. A hungry cat and a dog wanting to go for a walk have no difficulty in telling their human owners what they want. The body language of our pets conveys a great deal of information that we read subconsciously. They, of course, read our body language in the same way. However, for many people, this is not enough.

Is it possible for you and your pet to communicate psychically? I believe the answer is "yes," but with a few provisos. Your pet will be overjoyed at the prospect of communicating with you in this way. However, for communication to be effective it is important that you and your pet love each other and enjoy a close relationship. If your pet is a guard dog and spends most of his life chained to a kennel in your backyard, you are unlikely to have developed the relationship to the extent where psychic communication is possible. Obviously, there are exceptions, but usually strong bonds of love are essential for regular intuitive communication. You must be prepared to quieten your mind and listen. You need to be patient, respectful and open. There is no right or wrong way of doing it. Simply relax and allow it to happen.

Dr. Rupert Sheldrake postulates that there is a "morphic bond" that connects individual members of a group, even when they are widely separated. These bonds are not limited to members of the same family or group, and can occur between animals of different species, such as between humans and pets. The morphic fields are able to expand indefinitely, creating "channels for telepathic communication."[11]

The exercises in this book will help you and your pet develop the natural, possibly latent, psychic potential that is inherent in all living things. As you experiment with them, you will gain increased respect for the wonders of nature, and will become even closer to your treasured pet. It is a highly rewarding journey.

There is in every animal's eye a dim image and a gleam of humanity, a flash of strange light, through which their life looks at and up to our great mystery of command over them, and claims the fellowship of the creature, if not of the soul.
—JOHN RUSKIN

/

The Amazing Natural Talents of Animals

All living things are products of evolution. Gradual changes have taken place over millions of years, and each species has evolved in different ways. Consequently, although our pets live in the same world as we do, they see and experience it in different ways. Dogs, for instance, live in a world of smells. They also hear much more than we do. But they are partially colorblind, and their lives are much grayer than ours.

It is important to realize that many of the amazing things that animals do are not psychic in nature, but are related to their different natural abilities.

Back in the first century C.E., Pliny the Elder wrote about the horrifying ability of the numbfish to paralyze anyone who came too close to it. This was seventeen centuries before electricity was discovered, and the numbfish's abilities must have appeared supernatural. Nowadays, the numbfish is called an electric ray. It is able to generate a ninety-volt, high-amperage current. This is powerful, but is nothing compared to the incredible 550 volts generated by the electric eel.

We, like other animals, respond to stimuli that are significant to us, and ignore many others. Other animals may have the same senses that we have, but use them in different ways and in different degrees, depending on their natural abilities.

Dogs and cats, for example, have far greater hearing abilities than we have. Cats have a hearing range of between sixty and sixty-five thousand cycles per second. Dogs can hear between fifteen and fifty thousand, while we humans hear at about twenty thousand.

It used to be thought that elephants communicated telepathically when they were in difficulty or distress. However, it is now known that they call to each other at a level well below what the human ear can hear. The hearing range of elephants is between five and eighteen thousand cycles per second. Consequently, they are able to communicate over long distances using infrasound that is below the hearing range of most animals. It begins with a low rumble in the elephant's throat, which is amplified by a hollow area immediately below the forehead and directed outward. Elephants who are miles away are able to hear it and come to the distressed elephant's aid.[1]

Frogs have an extremely specialized sense of hearing. All they hear are the sounds of potential enemies or partners. This is all they actually need to hear. They find their prey using their keen sense of sight.[2]

Animals frequently have much stronger senses of smell than we have. When a cat, for example, decides to make friends with a stranger, it will rub its face and body against the person's legs, depositing an odor that helps it to recognize the person in the future. Wild cats also rub against each other in the same way, gaining feelings of security from the scent of the group. Cats use special scent glands at their temples, base of the tail, and at the corners of their mouth to swap scents with us. Cats want the people in their lives to have a familiar scent. This makes them feel secure, and makes their humans feel wanted.[3] Interestingly, cats will not rub themselves against people they do not like.[4]

Dogs possess a remarkable sense of smell that they inherited from their wolf ancestors. Humans possess some five million olfactory sensory cells that we use to smell with. This is nothing compared to what dogs have. A dachshund has about 125 million of these cells, while a sheepdog has 220 million. A bloodhound's sense of smell is one million times stronger than ours.[5]

When a human walks barefoot, he leaves one hundred-billionths of an ounce of sweat in each footprint. Any dog can track this tiny quantity with what appears to be supernatural accuracy. A bloodhound's sense of smell is so incredibly sensitive and accurate that it has the distinction of being "the only animal whose 'testimony' can be used as evidence in United States courts."[6] The dog's sense of smell is still the most effective way of locating people buried in snow avalanches. Sound detectors and other devices have a part to play, but are slow and cumbersome compared to "sniffer" dogs.

Some animals deliberately leave their scent in certain places to mark off their territory. Dogs, of course, do this with their feces and urine. Incidentally, dogs scatter the dirt with their paws after defecating. This is because they have sweat glands between their toes, and this action allows them to add another scent to the scene.

Ants travel in single file, following the scent left behind by an ant who has earlier found a source of food.

Salmon use their strong sense of smell to return to the river where they were born. They can sense the specific water, even if the river forks along the way. If they accidentally take the wrong fork they quickly become aware of it, and drift back downstream until they sense the smell again. They will then take the correct fork that leads them home.

The eyesight of many animals is much more acute than ours. Birds of prey are alert to the slightest movement in the landscape below them because they are using a much larger part of the spectrum of light than we are. There are even animals who can see the infrared part of the spectrum. The pit viper is an example of this. Even the humble goldfish has a vision that ranges from ultraviolet to far-red.[7]

Many animals are sensitive to magnetic fields. This explains some of the incredible abilities of migratory birds, homing pigeons, honeybees, and even the lowly snail. This also explains how whales are able to travel thousands of miles in their annual migrations.

Magnetism is the explanation for the famous migration of some one hundred million Monarch butterflies from Mexico to Carmel in California each year. The insects who make the journey are several generations distant from the ones who migrated the previous year, yet they are able to return to a specific tree once occupied by their ancestor. Because their bodies contain minute quantities of magnetite, scientists believe that these butterflies are using a combination of the sun's position and the Earth's magnetic field to enable them to travel the two-and-a-half thousand miles to California each year.

Magnetite is also found in the bodies of many other animals, including tuna, turtles, birds, and mice. Research is still going on into the role of magnetite in so many different animals. Obviously the ability of these animals to detect the Earth's magnetic field is extremely useful to them.

Of course, this talent can sometimes be dangerous. It appears that mass whale strandings occur when whales get caught up in areas of low magnetism that lead from the sea to the shore.[8] Apparently, whales use invisible magnetic contour lines as highways to travel along. Exactly how they do this is not yet known.

Animals communicate with each other in a variety of ways. Honeybees use a dance to tell the other bees where good sources of nectar and pollen can be found.

Although we cannot hear it with our ears, fish talk to each other incessantly. This was discovered during World War II when hydrophones were placed underwater to give advance warning of the approach of German submarines. To the surprise of everyone, a variety of groaning, clicking, and barking noises were heard. Until then, it was believed that the sea was a silent world. One evening in Chesapeake Bay, all the microphones recorded sounds that alerted the authorities. Huge quantities of depth charges were dropped into the bay. The following morning, no debris was found from any submarines, but the bay was littered with the bodies of dead fish.[9]

Birds sing for a variety of reasons. Sometimes it is to tell other birds of their location. At other times it is to advise the bird's mate about something. It may even be for some emotional reason that we do not yet understand.

Everything we have discussed here has been considered "psychic" at one time or another. However, it can all be explained logically. Consequently, we need to be careful when applying a paranormal explanation to the activities of any animal.

As humans, we tend to say that the remarkable activities of animals are simply "instinct." Many people find it hard to accept that animals have the power of thought, and can think, ponder, remember, imagine, create, make decisions, and act on them. Even the humble honeybee has this ability.

For some two hundred years, bumblebees have pollinated the alfalfa crops in North America. These bumblebees lived in the hedgerows and forest edges. However, as modern farming methods have virtually eliminated the hedgerows and forests, the bumblebees have been replaced by honeybees that apiarists are able to move from place to place.

Unfortunately, though, the alfalfa blossoms have spring-loaded anthers that flick the pollen onto the bees. This works well with bumblebees, but the small honeybees quickly learn that they receive a sharp jolt if they approach the alfalfa blossoms in the normal way.

Consequently, many honeybees ignore the alfalfa blossoms and search for nectar elsewhere. However, in areas where there is no other source of nectar, the bees have devised a system of removing the nectar from the side of the flower, which means they avoid the sharp flick from the anthers.[10]

Is this thought or instinct? Obviously, the honeybees have learned from experience that they can be hurt, and even trapped, by the alfalfa. The obvious solution is to simply avoid the alfalfa blossoms. This is what they do when substitutes are available. However, the bees appear to have thought about the situation and developed an alternative method of extracting the nectar. Of course, there may be another, as yet unknown, explanation, but this seems to be a sign of intelligence and thought. If a bee has this ability, imagine the potential of your pet.

All of these are natural talents that different animals possess. However, animals also possess psychic abilities. For instance, many animals are able to telepathically communicate with each other. A pack of wolves hunting their prey are able to communicate their intentions to each other in an uncanny fashion. Each wolf seems to know what the other wolves are thinking as they plan and capture their prey. It is as if someone was watching from above and directing the entire scene. A school of fish will all turn simultaneously as if following a silent command. Flocks of birds operate in the same way. How do they know the exact moment and direction to turn in?

Animals are also able to use clairvoyance. How are animals able to find their way home over long distances in unknown places? Faced with a fork in the road, they unerringly choose the right one.

Josef Schwarzl, a San Jose mechanic, owes his life to the clairvoyant talents of Toby, his golden Labrador. One day, while working alone, Josef was overcome with carbon-monoxide fumes from a car's exhaust. At the same time, Toby, who was four miles away at home, suddenly became agitated and insisted that he be let out the front door. Josef's mother opened the door, and the dog immediately raced toward the garage where his master lay unconscious. Josef's mother followed in her car and arrived in time to call emergency. Josef recovered in hospital, his life saved by the clairvoyancy of Toby.[11]

Precognition, or the ability to see into the future, is common with many animals. Dr. J. B. Rhine wrote that among his case reports of "unusual behavior in animals there are a fair number of cases in which the reaction is taken to be premonitory."[12]

A well-known example of this is the ability of rats to desert a ship that is shortly doomed to sink. How do they know? Animals usually know when an earthquake is about to occur. They may be able to learn of this through subtle changes that we are not yet aware of, but the ability of rats to know whether or not a ship will make it to the next port defies any explanation other than precognition.

Animals frequently know when a disaster is about to occur. Mr. A. H. Crowther experienced this when he received a phone call telling him that the Des Moines River was about to flood. He went to help a local farmer round up his pigs and cattle and take them to high ground. As they were doing this, they noticed a mother possum, with her young on her back, climbing up the hill. They then saw a woodchuck making the same trip. Shortly after that they saw a mother skunk getting her family away from the river. These animals were followed by a rabbit and a fat raccoon, all heading uphill.[13]

In 1989, Jim Berkland, a geologist in Santa Clara County, California, predicted the Lomo Prieta earthquake. He did this using a variety of methods, including combining the statistics of tides with the positions of the sun, moon, and the Earth. However, his most useful method was observation of the number of advertisements for lost cats in the local newspapers. Berkland says that after a decade of observation, he has noticed that cats tend to disappear shortly before volcanic activity occurs.[14]

The first recorded instance of animals behaving strangely before an earthquake dates back to 373 B.C.E. In that year, Helice, a city in Greece, was destroyed by an earthquake and fell into the sea. The Greek historian Diodorus Siculus wrote that rats, snakes, weasels, centipedes, worms, and beetles had headed inland in huge numbers before the eruption.[15]

Even the ancient Romans were aware that the behavior of animals changes before a major earthquake. Pliny the Elder commented on this in the second book of his *Historia Naturalis*: "Even the birds do not stay sitting free of fear."[16]

If such information has been known for more than two thousand years, isn't it strange that scientists take such little notice of it? It is not as if the animals do not make their fear known. Before a 1783 earthquake in Messina, the howling of dogs in the street was so loud that the authorities issued orders to kill them.[17]

It was the Chinese who were the first to successfully predict a major earthquake, using a variety of methods, but with special emphasis on animal behavior. The successful prediction of the Haicheng earthquake of February 4, 1975, proved once and for all that what had previously been considered superstition was in fact real. Unfortunately, the Chinese did not continue practicing what they had learned. On July 28, 1976, an estimated 655,000 people were killed in the Tangshan earthquake.[18]

In his book *When the Snakes Awake*, Helmut Tributsch lists a large number of recorded instances of unusual animal behavior before an earthquake. These include seabirds flying inland, chickens roosting late, cattle late or reluctant to enter their stalls, deer and other game coming out of the woods and even approaching people, ants becoming agitated, fish jumping out of the water, roosters crowing persistently at night, birds flocking together and circling, cats crying and disappearing, bears and snakes coming out of hibernation, and the sudden disappearance of flies.[19]

This sort of behavior has been observed for thousands of years, and is another example of a talent that animals possess. If we humans ever possessed it, somehow we lost it over the last few thousand years. How do animals do it? At present, no one knows, although there are many theories. There are changes in the Earth's magnetic fields before earthquakes, and many animals will be aware of these. There are also changes in the Earth's electrical fields. Some animals may be able to hear the very beginnings of an earthquake long before humans are aware that anything is wrong. Some animals may even be aware of movements in the Earth's crust. Others may be able to smell Earth gases. Perhaps these animals are using their natural precognitive talents.

The skills of telepathy, clairvoyance, and precognition are also inherent in humans, even though many people try to deny them.

Two dogs, for instance, can communicate telepathically with each other. This is communication within a species. However, it is also possible for one species of animals to communicate telepathically with another species. This means that you have the ability to exchange telepathic messages with your pet. In fact, you have probably done this many times already, without being aware of it. This book will teach you how to do it consciously in a way that will benefit both you and your pet. The relationship you have will be enriched and become even closer as a result.

My daughter's experiences with Clyde, our cat, are examples of this. Other examples include the eminent nineteenth-century actor, William Terries, who was stabbed to death in London. At the time of his death, his fox terrier, who was in Bedford, began running about, howling and yelping with rage and fear.[20]

Probably the most remarkable instance that I have come across involves a dog called Hector. His case involves precognition as well as telepathy. He was observed at the Vancouver docks boarding four different ships. The next day, the SS *Hanley* left port for Japan, and Hector was found on it. The crew were delighted to have the dog on board, but Hector remained aloof. However, he became more animated when the ship neared Japan. The ship dropped anchor in Yokohama, close to a Dutch ship. A small boat was launched from the Dutch ship and Hector jumped into the sea and swam across to it. Hector's master was on this small boat. How did Hector manage to do this? First of all, he must have decided which of four ships to smuggle himself on to in Vancouver, and secondly, he somehow divined that the Dutch ship containing his master would be in port at the exact same time as the SS *Hanley*.[21]

When I play with my cat, who knows whether she isn't amusing herself with me more than I am with her?
—MONTAIGNE (1533–1592)

2

The Mysterious Cat

Dogs were domesticated some fourteen thousand years ago, but our relationship with cats dates back only half that length of time. The earliest evidence of domesticated cats dates back seven thousand years and was discovered by Alaine le Brun, an archaeologist, in Khirokitia, Cyprus.

Cats were not considered valuable to people until we became an agricultural society and began storing food for later use. Cats suddenly became welcome as they dealt efficiently with the rats and mice.

It is not surprising that cats were venerated and worshipped in the past. Cats were considered sacred in ancient Egypt, and it was illegal to kill them. Huge numbers of them were mummified, and as recently as a hundred years ago the mummies were ground up and sold as fertilizer.[1]

Cats convey a sense of mystery, an aloofness, and an independence that constantly makes their owners wonder who, exactly, owns who. An old saying with much truth in it says dogs have masters, but cats have staff. Cats never surrender any part of their individuality. The fact that they successfully live in two worlds at the same time make them the most fascinating of pets. Your cat might be sleeping peacefully on your lap at one moment, and yet a short time later go outside and be protective of its territory and skilled at catching its prey.

Cats are extremely well adapted for the world they live in. They possess flexible backbones that enable them to swivel their bodies in ways that are impossible for other animals. This enables them to arch their backs while stretching, and to curl themselves up into tight balls while sleeping. Their success as hunters is partly due to their powerful hind legs and incredible agility. However, they also use hearing, taste, touch, smell, and sight. Of these, the most important is their incredible sense of sight.

Cats are able to see clearly, even in almost total darkness. The eyes of cats reflect light back to the retina. This increases the intensity of any available light, and also makes their eyes appear to glow in the dark. The eyes of cats are unusual in that the field of vision of each eye slightly overlaps the other. This is called binocular vision. It allows cats to locate their prey with incredible accuracy because each eye sends different messages about size and distance to the brain.

Cats are covered with hair, of course, and some of these have become specially modified to act as sensory organs. The whiskers are the obvious ones, but cats also have sensory hairs above the eyes and on the sides of their heads. These are attached to nerves in the skin and are extremely sensitive. Incidentally, cats' whiskers are the first hairs to develop in the womb.

Cats have a good sense of hearing, and can pick up much higher-pitched sounds than we can. This is because their natural prey, such as rodents and birds, make sounds that are high-pitched. Their ears contain a dozen muscles that enable it to move up to 180 degrees in the direction of any sound. Their ears also contain semicircular canals that provide them with their unerring sense of balance. This enables cats to land on their feet after a fall.

Cats have a sense of smell that is estimated to be almost four times better than that of humans. They also have a scent organ on the roof of their mouths, known as Jacobsen's organ. Traces of scents are picked up from air on the tongue, and are then pressed against Jacobsen's organ, which transfers it to the brain. This sense, which appears to be a mixture of taste and smell, is something that we humans lack completely.

It is not known exactly how or why cats purr. It is thought that membranes close to the vocal cords vibrate to create the comforting sound of a purr. When cats purr, we normally feel that they are contented. However, cats also purr when they are sick or injured. Researchers at the

Fauna Communications Research Institute in North Carolina believe that purring acts in a similar manner to ultrasound, and helps the bones and other organs to heal and grow. In other words, purring aids natural healing.[2]

The psychic abilities of cats have been known for thousands of years. The ancient Egyptians called the cat *mau*, "the seer." The Egyptian word *mau* means "to see." This appears to mean not only the ability to see into the future, but also the ability to see things that most of us cannot.

It appears that cats are highly sensitive to ghosts, and we will be discussing this in chapter 7. Cats are also sensitive to magnetic and electrical disturbances in the atmosphere. In the days leading up to a major earthquake in northern Italy in May 1876, people noticed the strange behavior of the animals. Wild deer came down from the hills, cats left home, dogs barked, and even rats and mice came out into the open in broad daylight.[3]

There is an interesting case in which two cats saved the lives of their master before another major earthquake in Italy, this time in Messina. A merchant in that town noticed his cats scratching wildly at the door to his room. When he opened it, they raced to the front door and began scratching there, too. He let them out and followed them through the streets to an open field. Even here, they appeared upset and "frantically tore and scratched at the grass."[4] Shortly after this, the first shock of the earthquake came and the merchant's house, along with many others, fell to the ground.

Cats are obviously extremely good at predicting earthquakes. Various reasons for this have been suggested. Perhaps they are so aware of the Earth's vibrations that they can sense them even before instruments are able to detect them. It is possible that they respond to the rapid increase in static electricity that precedes earthquakes. Maybe they are extremely aware of any sudden changes in the Earth's magnetic field. Or perhaps this ability is a psychic one, as cats are undoubtedly extremely psychic.

An interesting example, in which a cat's premonition saved her kitten, occurred at St. Augustine's Church in London during the Second World War. The vicar had adopted a homeless cat, which he called Faith. She loved the church and sometimes even attended services, sitting upright and paying attention throughout. In 1940, Faith gave birth to a kitten, which the family called Panda. On September 6, Faith became obviously agitated, and carefully examined every room in the vicarage. Finally, she took Panda and disappeared. The vicar found them sitting in a small opening in a wall below ground level, three floors below. He carried the kitten back upstairs four times, but each time Faith immediately took him back. Finally, the vicar gave up, and took the cat's basket down to its new home. Three days later, while the vicar was out, the vicarage was bombed and burned to the ground. The vicar called out to Faith and heard a faint reply. Firemen were able to release the unharmed mother and baby just a few minutes before the floor collapsed into the flames.[5]

My sister, Penny, reminded me of an example of a cat's precognition that I had forgotten. When we were children our parents rented a vacation home every year at a seaside resort. The elderly woman who owned the house had a large black cat. The first year we stayed there, the woman greeted us when we arrived, introduced us to her cat and gave detailed instructions on how to look after it. Half an hour after she left, the cat disappeared and did not reappear until the day we were packing up to return home. We had spent the entire vacation worrying about her, but she appeared to be in perfect health and had been well looked after.

The following year, the exact same thing happened. The cat waited until we were settled in and then left for three weeks, again returning the day that we left. She did this every year for five years. None of us caught as much as a glimpse of her during the three weeks we stayed at the house. Yet somehow this cat knew exactly when her mistress was going to return, and arrived on the doorstep about an hour before she did.

The ancient Egyptians originally domesticated African wild cats to help control the rats that were decimating their supplies of grain. Over a period of time, cats became more and more important in Egyptian society, until eventually they were worshipped. Bastet, the goddess of fertility, was depicted in two forms: either with the body of a woman and the head of a cat, or as a sitting cat. Because the Egyptians believed that the eyes of cats could hang on to the sun's rays, Bastet was also considered responsible for the power, strength, and warmth of the sun. One of the names given to the sun god Ra was "The Great Cat." Bastet was closely associated with Isis. Consequently, cats were an important part of every temple of Isis. It is possible that the distribution of cats throughout Europe and the Middle East began as the cult of Isis grew and their temples gradually expanded as well.[6]

The incredible power that cats wielded was demonstrated vividly during a war between Persia and Egypt. According to legend, the Persian king gave all of his frontline soldiers cats to use as shields. Rather than kill these cats, the Egyptians surrendered.[7]

A similar story is told about the Persian king Hormus, who was being attacked by an army of some three hundred thousand men. A mysterious old man appeared and told the king that he would defeat the enemy in a single day if he could find a cat-faced man to lead his army. The king frantically searched for such a man. Eventually, a mountaineer with a face that was distinctly catlike was found. The king made him a general and put him in charge of his army. Even though the Persians had only twelve thousand men, with this man in command, they defeated the enemy in just one day.[8]

It is interesting to speculate how the cat, formerly revered and worshipped, gradually became associated with evil and the devil. Perhaps this happened because cats are so at home in the night, the time of day that medieval people feared most. Their silent comings and goings made people wonder if they were possibly spying for the devil. Consequently, in 1484, Pope Innocent VII initiated an inquisition against cats, and millions of cats were tortured and killed.

In the Middle Ages it was also believed that witches were able to put their souls into the bodies of black cats. Superstitious people were only too willing to believe stories such as this, and began persecuting the cats, as well as witches. People accepted that these women had made a pact with the devil. They were believed to have supernatural powers that they used to gain revenge, start plagues, dry up the milk of suckling mothers, and cause impotence or sterility. No wonder they were feared. Black cats became an omen of bad luck and misfortune; many were killed, because the population believed that by doing so they were actually killing witches.[9] Even today many people associate black cats with bad luck.

There are many stories told of how witches were able to turn themselves into cats. One well-known story concerns a Scotsman nameded William Montgomery. He was awakened one night in 1718 by the sounds of screeching cats. When he went outside to see what was going on, a number of the cats tried to scratch him. Infuriated by this, Montgomery picked up an axe to defend himself. He killed two cats and injured some of the others. The following morning, two elderly women in his village were found dead in their beds, and another woman had an injured leg that she could not explain. William Montgomery believed that these women were witches who had temporarily become cats in order to attack him.[10]

Cats were persecuted in China, also. This is because people involved in black magic used cats to steal money and harm people in various ways. The problem became so great that in 598 C.E., Emperor Khai-hwang ordered anyone involved with cat-specters to be banished to the harshest regions of the empire.[11] The ancient Chinese also believed that cats were able to give advance warning of approaching demons in the dark.[12]

It is strange how superstitions vary from country to country. In England it is considered a sign of good luck if a black cat comes toward you. A black cat crossing your path is considered a sign of bad luck in America. Sir Winston Churchill considered his black cat to be a good omen. A tiny black kitten arrived at 10 Downing Street on the day that Winston Churchill gave an address to the Conservative Party annual conference in 1953. This address was an extremely important one for Sir Winston as people were saying that he was too old and should retire. His speech was extremely successful, and Sir Winston named the cat Margate, which was the name of the place where the conference was held.

King Charles I also had a favorite cat, which also happened to be black. When it died, he allegedly said, "My luck is gone." The very next day he was arrested.[13]

Amazingly enough, rats were the ultimate savior of cats in Europe. Soldiers returning from the Crusades accidentally brought black rats with them. In less than fifty years these rats had spread throughout Europe, destroying much of the harvested grain and spreading plague in their wake. Suddenly, cats were needed again.

When I was growing up, we always had at least one, and usually two cats. As a child my favorite cat was Ting, a Siamese. Possibly because he used my bedroom window to get in and out of the house, and also slept on my bed every night, we developed a special bond. He was good-natured and affectionate, and tolerated my childish games and high spirits. He would tell me when he had had enough by jumping into my arms, effectively ending the game. Most mornings he would wake me up by playing with my feet. If he was ready to go to bed and I wasn't already there, he would pat at my legs to remind me that it was bedtime. One night, he arrived home with a large goose. This made us think he was an amazing hunter. However, after he died, we discovered that he had stolen the goose from a neighbor's kitchen table.

Ting never showed any interest in the telephone until Meredith, my younger sister, went into the hospital for a lengthy stay. Back in the sixties it was not easy for Meredith to call us from hospital, but we always knew whenever she was calling as Ting would be on the telephone table, rubbing his face against the instrument before we could answer it.

Ting also saved the life of our Labrador dog, Bruce. In the course of a fight with a German shepherd, Bruce had half of one ear bitten off. Ting raced inside and agitatedly alerted us to the danger. He then led the way back to the street where Bruce was lying helpless in a pool of blood while the German shepherd continued his attack. If Ting had not alerted us, Bruce would probably have died from loss of blood.

Of course, cats have been saving the lives of people ever since humans and cats became friends. During the Second World War, it quickly became apparent that cats knew about bombing raids well before the German planes were detected by radar. They would race to the bomb shelters, and people would quickly follow. It is impossible to estimate how many lives were saved in this way.

Unlike dogs, cats are solitary creatures. Their apparent aloofness is alluring to some people, but annoying to others. Cats possess an extreme psychic awareness, using this and their other five senses to remain constantly aware of everything that is happening in the world around them. They are constantly receiving information mentally, physically, and psychically, and this information is immediately acted upon.

Cats use their entire body to communicate their desires and feelings. They use body language all the time to achieve their aims. They will dance in front of their owners and rub against their legs, with their tails high and twitching. They'll purr while doing this to add another element to the equation.

When we had Siamese cats I always looked forward to returning home from work because of the welcome they would give me. As soon as they saw me they would run toward me with their tails high, meowing their pleasure at my return. They would rub against my legs, dancing and showing off in delight.

Cats are superb at commanding attention from the humans in their lives. They are good actors when required, also. Our huge tabby cat somehow managed to look thin and in need of nourishment whenever he thought it was mealtime.

Cats appear to communicate with other cats using a mixture of body language, sounds, and telepathy. A good example of this concerns the last week in the life of Lucky, a stray cat who was adopted by a loving family. Lucky was always extremely protective of her territory and quickly chased away any cats that dared to enter her property. A family living a few houses away took in a cat called Sophie. Unfortunately, Sophie was not as fortunate as Lucky, as she was put out every night and fed only spasmodically.

Lucky's family was amazed to find that a week before Lucky died, Sophie, an extremely timid cat, began visiting Lucky, even venturing inside the house. The two cats had lengthy vocal conversations every time Sophie visited.

On the Saturday morning when Lucky paid her final visit to the veterinarian, Sophie arrived early and had the usual long conversation. Finally, the two cats touched noses, and Sophie left. Later in the day, when the family returned home, Sophie was in the driveway waiting for them. She ran to meet the car and rolled on her back in the same way that Lucky used to do. She came into the house, and stayed. It would appear that Lucky knew her days were numbered, and had asked Sophie to take her place.[14]

Dr. J. B. Rhine conducted a number of scientific experiments with cats during his time at Duke University. One that particularly intrigued me involved a psychology student who was able to astral travel. This student had a seven-week-old kitten that was only happy when the student was in the same room as her. Whenever he left the room, the cat became upset and meowed constantly, stopping only when he returned.

Researchers recorded all of this until a pattern was established. The student was then taken to a room that was well away from the cat and astral traveled back to see how she was. The kitten became upset, as usual, when he left but stopped crying when she became aware that the student was psychically present.[15] It is not hard to astral travel.[16] If you learn how to do it, you will be able to conduct this experiment with your own cat.

Another experiment, conducted by Helmut Schmidt in 1970, was to determine the psychokinetic potential of a cat. A cat was placed in a cold shed that was spasmodically heated by a lamp attached to a random number generator. Consequently, the lamp turned on and off in an unpredictable manner. By chance alone, the lamp should have remained on for half of the time the cat was in the shed. In fact it stayed on for much longer periods than could be explained by chance. Using psychokinesis, the cat was influencing the amount of time the lamp stayed on.[17]

Cat owners instinctively know that to become really close to their pets they have to communicate with them telepathically, as well as in every other way. Cats can understand more than one hundred common words, such as "dinner," "yes," "play," and "beautiful."[18] In fact, I believe that they understand much more than that, as they are constantly reading our minds. When we speak to them, they gain much more than friendly sounds, as they are also receiving the pictures we constantly create in our minds. Cats enjoy being spoken to, as it means that they are being included in your world.

They also observe your body language closely. A cat that is resting on your lap will be able to tell the difference between when you are moving position to become more comfortable, or shifting position because you are about to get up. Cats are aware of much more than we think possible. This is because they are constantly using all six senses. When we use our sixth sense in dealing with them, we can achieve a closeness that cannot be achieved in any other way. It takes time and practice, but the rewards can be incredible.

All cats are psychic, but the Japanese bobtail is supposed to be the most psychic cat of all.[19] This cat also welcomes you home with one paw raised in the air, exactly like Meneki-neko, the famous porcelain cat that is used as a talisman to attract money and good fortune.

Telepathy with Your Cat

Choose a time when neither of you are tired. Avoid meal times, as your cat is likely to be preoccupied with food if that time of day is approaching.

Sit down somewhere comfortable and stroke your cat. It makes no difference if your cat is sitting on your lap, or sitting or lying down beside you. Do not say anything out loud, but think loving thoughts as you stroke your pet. He or she is likely to respond to both your thoughts and actions.

Gradually, stop stroking your cat, but continue thinking loving thoughts. Your cat should continue purring and may turn to look at you. After a minute or two, stop thinking loving thoughts and silently ask your pet a question. It makes no difference what question you ask. Typical examples are: "Do you love me?" "Are you happy?" or "What would you like me to do for you?"

You may wish to close your eyes while waiting for a response from your pet. It is not necessary to do this, but many people find it helpful, particularly when starting to communicate telepathically with their pets. Be patient and see what thoughts pop into your mind.

Your pet might respond in a physical way. Our tabby cat, Clyde, always answered the question "Do you love me?" by rubbing his face against our hands. If you think "Would you like food?" your cat is likely to mew a response and lead the way to the kitchen.

Physical responses are easy to gauge. Telepathic replies can sometimes be difficult to measure. Your cat may be feeling sleepy and be reluctant to play the communication game. You may subconsciously resist the reply, or may simply not recognize it when it appears. The reply might be a feeling or sensation, rather than anything specific. Sometimes you might receive a clear picture. The results can vary enormously.

It is natural to feel disappointed when the results are not what you expected. Try to dismiss these feelings, as your pet will sense them. Be grateful for any replies that your cat sends, and be understanding when nothing comes through.

Repeat this exercise as frequently as possible. You will find that your cat will look forward to it as much as you do, as he or she will be aware that you are doing it so that the two of you can gain an even closer relationship.

Sending Thoughts

This experiment should be done well away from normal feeding times. To begin with, your cat should be in the same room as you. Later on, it does not matter where he or she is.

Sit down comfortably, close your eyes, and take ten deep breaths. Picture yourself, in your mind, feeding your pet. See yourself getting the food, placing it in a dish, and putting it down where your cat eats. In your mind, watch your cat eating the food.

Open your eyes, and go through the scene again. Experience it as vividly as you can. Not everyone can "see" scenes clearly in their imagination. However, you might sense it happening, you might feel your cat rubbing against your legs, you might hear your cat purring or meowing in your mind. It makes no difference how you relive the scene in your imagination, just as long as you remain focused on it for at least five minutes.

Pay no attention to your cat while doing this. It might be helpful to face away so that you are not watching him or her while thinking about food.

If your cat has received your thought, he or she will have woken up and will be rubbing against you, meowing, or doing other actions to tell you that it is time for food.

Naturally, you will have to produce a treat of some sort to reward your cat for picking up your thoughts. You should also reward yourself in some way, as you will have proved the reality of interspecies communication.

Once you have succeeded with this experiment, try repeating it when your cat is not in the same room as you. You will find that it makes no difference where your cat is, indoors or out. Once your cat has picked up your thoughts about food once, distance will make no difference in his or her ability to do it again.

The advantage that this experiment has over many others is that your cat is unlikely to ignore it, unless he or she is in an extremely deep sleep or has just eaten.

Coming Home Test

This is a test in precognition. If your cat regularly waits for you to arrive home, vary the time you return for three or four days. Ask a friend or family member to observe your cat to see if he or she knows when you are returning. Your friend should record everything your cat does in the hour or so before the time you agreed to return. Do not return at the exact time you stated. Allow five or ten minutes either side of the time you indicated. This is to eliminate the possibility that your cat is picking up telepathic cues from your friend that you are about to return home.

Come to Me Test

This is a test in telepathy that you can do when you want your cat for some reason. Instead of calling him or her, sit down comfortably, close your eyes, and think about your cat. Summon him or her to you mentally. It is unlikely that you will have to do this for more than five minutes before your cat will arrive.

The Food Bowl Test

This is a test that was devised by Dr. Karlis Osis, a retired animal behaviorist. He is a former director of research at the American Society for Psychical Research. In the 1950s, Dr. Osis worked at the Parapsychology Laboratory at Duke University with Dr. Rhine. Dr. Osis conducted a series of tests with cats in a home environment, using his ten-year-old daughter, Gunta. Gunta would place an equal amount of food into two identical dishes and then mentally will each cat to choose the dish that she had previously selected as the target. Over a number of trials, Gunta was able to successfully influence the actions of several cats.[20]

You can replicate this test exactly. Choose two identical dishes and put the same amount of cat food in each of them. Place one of these to the left of the doorway your cat will be using, and place the other the same distance to the right.

Decide which dish you want your cat to choose. Think about this dish. Repeat to yourself over and over again, "I want my cat to choose the dish on the left," for instance. Call your cat (if he or she has not already arrived), and keep on repeating the words in your mind.

Keep records and see if, over a period of time, your cat responds to your thoughts.

The more I see of men, the better I like dogs.
—FREDERICK THE GREAT OF PRUSSIA (1712–1786)

3

Man's Best Friend

Arguably, dogs are the animals that are most loved by humans. When British broadcaster Martyn Lewis wrote a book called *Cats in the News*, he received letters from people telling him that there are 600,000 more dogs in Britain than there are cats. Therefore, why did he write a book on cats before writing one about dogs?[1]

Dogs have been man's best friend for some twenty thousand years.[2] At the end of the Ice Age they were rivals for food, but since then they have enjoyed a mutually supportive relationship. The remains of a dog were found at the Stone Carr Stone Age settlement in Yorkshire, England. These remains date back to around 7500 B.C.E. Hounds were depicted on a tomb wall of Senbi, Prince of

Cusae, and date back to 4000 B.C.E. By the start of the Christian era, dogs were frequently depicted in the art and ceramics of Assyria, China, Greece, and Italy, showing that they had become an important and essential part of everyday life.[3]

The friendly, loving, forgiving nature of dogs, combined with their intelligence and loyalty, has made them popular pets all around the world.

Dog owners receive many benefits from the association, including some that may appear surprising. For instance, it has been claimed that dogs improve people's marriages. A study at Indiana University found that people could resolve their marital difficulties more easily when their pet dog was in the room. Apparently, the couples showed less aggression when their dog was present, and their heart rates and blood pressures stayed lower.[4] Scientists have shown that the blood pressure of humans decreases when a dog enters a room.[5] Consequently, the blood pressure of people who have a dog living in the house is permanently lowered.

In fact, most dog owners consider their pet to be a family member (99 percent), and more than half of all domestic dogs sleep on the same bed as a human member of the household (56 percent). The same survey also reported that 64 percent gave their dog tidbits from the table, 86 percent shared snacks with their dog, and 54 percent celebrated their dog's birthday.[6]

Rameses the Great had four dogs, one of whom was allowed to sleep in his bed. Alexander the Great was also known to share his bed with his great mastiff, Peritas. Mary, Queen of Scots, slept with her miniature Skye Terrier while imprisoned in the Tower of London. (Some authorities describe her dog as a spaniel. Breeds were not as well defined in those days as they are now.) In fact, she even smuggled her dog to her execution in 1587. It was found in her voluminous dress after her death.[7] Queen Elizabeth I, the person who ordered Mary's execution, spent the last night of her life with a miniature spaniel, also. King Charles II also slept with his spaniels, and even gave them the name King Charles spaniels. Czar Peter the Great slept with Lissette, his Italian greyhound.

However, not everyone enjoys having a dog on his or her bed. General George Armstrong Custer had many arguments with his wife, Libbie, about allowing dogs on their bed. Finally, Libbie threatened to sleep elsewhere if her husband insisted on the presence of the dogs. Fortunately, they came to a compromise: when General Custer was at home, the dogs could stay in the bedroom as long as they slept on the floor. However, in the field, General Custer always shared his bed with Turk, a bulldog, and Blucher and Byron, his two greyhounds.

As well as being wonderful pets, many dogs work for their livings. They track down criminals, seek out drugs and explosives, round up sheep, and work as guide dogs for the blind. Some even work in highly unusual ways. Ninon de Lenclos was a famous seventeenth-century prostitute. She and her dog Raton were inseparable, and Ninon carried him everywhere with her. Ninon had a long and successful career as a prostitute, and this was partly due to Raton. Whenever she picked up any food that was sweet or fattening, Raton would bark until she put it down again.[8]

Although dogs are descended from the same species as wolves, coyotes, and jackals, they willingly gave up life in the wild for the benefits of domestication. Dogs are totally dependent on their human owners for survival. They enjoy following them around to maintain a close visual contact, and wait patiently for them to return home when they are away. They want to be in constant communication with their human masters. They love being talked to, patted, and stroked, and also desire a close intuitive relationship. This enables them to continue communicating with their masters, even when they are many miles apart.

The devotion of dogs is remarkable. One famous example of this dates back to the eruption of Vesuvius. Archaeologists excavating the ruins of ancient Pompeii found the fossilized remains of a small boy beside the body of a dead dog. The inscription on the bronze collar was still legible: "This dog has saved his little master three times—once from fire, once from drowning, once from thieves." One interesting fact about Pompeii is that although thousands of people perished, very few domestic animals died. Obviously, they were able to sense the impending disaster and escape. Yet this dog, who had already saved his master three times, must have sensed the danger but stayed with the boy anyway.[9]

Geoffrey Chaucer metaphorically described the love and devotion of dogs in *The Canterbury Tales*. The Widow of Bath described the behavior of a certain woman toward a man as "For as a spaynel she will on him lepe."

Napoleon Bonaparte was impressed by the loyalty of a soldier's dog. He wrote: "Suddenly I saw a dog emerging from under the greatcoat of a corpse. He rushed toward us, then returned to his retreat uttering mournful cries. He licked the face of his former master and darted toward us again; it seemed as if he was seeking aid and vengeance at the same time. Whether it was my state of mind, or the silence of the guns, the weather, the dog's act itself or I know not what, never has anything on a field of battle made such an impression on me . . . I had seen, dry-eyed, movements executed which resulted in the loss of a great number of our soldiers; but here and now, that dog moved me to tears."[10]

A more modern example of the loyalty and devotion of dogs occurred in 1975 when Mark Cooper took his German shepherd, Zorro, with him on a trip to Sierra Nevada. On the trip Mark fell eighty-five feet into a ravine, landing in a stream. When he regained consciousness, he became aware that Zorro was dragging him out of the water and up a steep bank. Friends found the pair and went for help, while Zorro lay on top of his master to keep him warm. The next day a helicopter picked Mark up, but forgot Zorro. Volunteers went out to find him and discovered him guarding Mark's backback. Ken-L Rations proclaimed Zorro "Dog Hero of the Year" for saving his master's life.[11]

When I lived in Scotland I used to attend as many events at the annual Edinburgh Festival as possible. I always parked my car close to the statue of Greyfriars Bobby, a small terrier whose story was made famous in the Walt Disney film *Greyfriars Bobby*. Bobby belonged to a shepherd known as "Auld Jock." The two of them regularly ate at the Greyfriars Dining Room, owned by a Mr. Traill.

Jock died in 1858 and was buried in Greyfriars Kirkyard. Bobby began his vigil beside the grave and would not move. Each time he was evicted, he would find a way back in. At one o'clock each day he would walk across to the Greyfriars Dining Room for a meal. The Traills tried to take him in, but Bobby always returned to his master's grave, remaining there for fourteen years.

At one time, the police arrested Bobby because he was an "unlicensed vagrant." Mr. Traill, the owner of the dining rooms, also appeared in court, accused of supporting the dog in his illegal activities because he continued to feed him. They appeared before Sir William Chambers, the Lord Provost. When Sir William heard the story, he offered to pay for Bobby's license for the rest of his life. He also had a special collar made that read: "Greyfriars Bobby, from the Lord Provost 1867. Licensed." This collar is now in the Huntley Museum in Edinburgh.

Bobby died in 1872 and was buried near the main entrance to the church. A group of Americans heard about Bobby and paid for a headstone for Auld Jock's grave. Baroness Burdett-Coutts, a society leader of the day, erected a drinking fountain and bronze statue of Bobby in Candlemaker Row, where it quickly became a tourist attraction. More than 125 years after his death, the loyalty and devotion of Bobby is still remembered.

When I was in Tokyo, I chanced upon the statue of a dog called Hachiko, at Shibuya station. Hachiko used to accompany his master, Dr. Eisaburo Ueno, to the railway station every morning, and would return there to greet him when he returned home. One day, Dr. Ueno died at work. Ha-chiko turned up as usual to meet his master and waited until midnight before returning home. Every day for the next ten years Hachiko returned to the railway station in the hope of greeting his master. When he died in 1935, a bronze statue was erected in his honor. Every year, on April 8, a special ceremony is held to honor his memory.

A more recent story from Cheshire, England, is just as moving. On Christmas Eve, 1999, Spot, a Border collie, left the home of his new owners and set out to find the grave of his former master. He had never been to the gravesite before, but unerringly traveled four miles to the cemetery at St. John's Church. He had to cross several main roads to do this. A policeman found him lying on top of his master's grave.[12]

The devotion that dogs have for their masters is well known. Sadly, humans do not always show the same trust or devotion to their pets.

One example of this occurred in thirteenth-century Wales in the village of Beddgelert (which means "grave of Gelert"). Gelert was a wolfhound owned by Prince Llywellyn.

One day the prince returned from a hunting trip and found Gelert covered with blood. The prince ran to his infant son's room and found the sheets were stained with blood. There was no sign of the child. Prince Llywellyn immediately thought that Gelert had killed his son. He took out his sword and killed the dog. Gelert's dying cry woke the son, who had been sleeping underneath some covering. Next to his son, Prince Llewellyn found the body of a large wolf. Far from killing his son, Gelert had saved his life by killing the wolf. The prince was full of remorse, but it was too late to save Gelert. This story became even better known in the nineteenth century when William Robert Spencer wrote a poem about the incident called *Beth Gelert*. Today, many tourists visit Gelert's grave in a field at Beddgelert, near Mount Snowdon in North Wales.[13]

Another example was told in the book *Dogs and Their Ways* by Rev. Charles Williams. Williams tells the story of a French merchant who had collected some money that was owed to him. He was returning home on horseback, with his dog running alongside. After some miles, the merchant paused to rest. He placed the money under a hedge, and lay down in the shade. When he got up again and recommenced his journey, his dog followed reluctantly, barking, howling, and eventually snapping at the heels of the horse. They crossed a small brook and the dog did not pause for a drink. The merchant thought that his dog had gone mad, and decided to put it out of its misery. He shot the dog, but failed to kill it. The dog tried to crawl toward his master. Sickened by the sight, the merchant remounted his horse and rode away, thinking that he would rather have lost his money than his dog. Suddenly he remembered that he had left the money under the hedge. He turned around and hurried back. His dog was under the hedge, guarding the money. He wagged his tail when his master returned, licked his hand, and died.

This example also shows the reasoning powers that dogs possess. This dog immediately understood that his master was accidentally leaving the money behind. He did everything in his power to tell his master this. Even after his master shot him, he returned to the money to protect it.

Sigmund Freud was extremely dependent on his chow, Jo-Fi, and used her to determine his patients' mental states. This is because the dog would lie down at differing distances from the patient, depending on the degree of stress the person was suffering.[14]

Dogs are renowned for their incredible sense of smell. More than 10 percent of a dog's brain is devoted to analyzing and processing smells. In the human brain less than 1 percent of it is dedicated to the same task.[15] Most dogs can detect even a single drop of blood in ten pints of water. Mexican drug smugglers offered $70,000 to anyone who would kill Rocky or Barco, two Belgian Malinois dogs who were experts at locating hidden drugs. Their skills resulted in more than 250 arrests and the seizure of more than 300 million dollars worth of drugs. Even more amazing is the 1 million dollars that Colombian drug dealers offered to anyone who would kill Winston, a Labrador retriever, who had cost them more than one billion dollars in seizures.[16]

In Denmark and Holland, sniffer dogs are also used to detect and trace gas leaks, and it is believed that they are more efficient and reliable than electronic devices.[17]

Their sense of smell is well-known. What is less known is that dogs are highly intuitive. My father-in-law was a sheep farmer. Whenever he was working with his sheep dogs, he had to focus solely on the actions he wanted his dogs to perform at that moment. As soon as he began thinking about the next move, his dogs would start performing it. Obviously, they were reading his mind rather than waiting for his whistled signals.

In Northern Ireland, a sniffer dog indicated a particular spot in a brick wall. Cemented deep inside was a rifle that had been hidden there twenty-five years earlier.[18] Obviously, this dog was not using his nose to locate the concealed weapon. Clairvoyancy is a more likely explanation.

Telepathy between dogs and their humans is extremely common. Dr. Rupert Sheldrake reported an incident in which telepathy saved the owner's life. A woman in the north of England was having major marital problems and decided to kill herself. Her dog and cats were sleeping in front of the fire when she went to the kitchen for water and Paracetamol. Suddenly, William, a Springer spaniel, raced up to her and snarled. He had not done this once in the previous fifteen years. The dog's "jowls were pulled completely back so that he was almost unrecognizable." The woman was terrified of her own dog. She replaced the lid on the bottle of tablets and returned to the sofa.

William followed her back and licked her face frantically, while his entire body wagged with happiness.[19]

In his book *Kinship with All Life*, author J. Allen Boone described an experience that occurred with a German shepherd dog he was looking after called Strongheart. One morning, Boone did not feel like working, and thought how pleasant it would be to take the dog for a walk in the hills. While he was still thinking about this, Strongheart bounded inside in a state of great excitement, licked Boone's hand, and then brought out his sweater, jeans, boots, and walking stick, one at a time. "Then bouncing, and swirling, he made it clear that he felt we should leave at once, and sooner if possible."[20] Boone had not said anything to Strongheart about going for a walk, but the dog had obviously read his mind.

Admittedly, Strongheart was an exceptionally intelligent dog who had been trained by the Army and later appeared in many films. Strongheart was the first animal movie star and was a huge box-office draw in the 1920s. Strongheart was an amazing animal, but he was not unique. All dogs are capable of reading the minds of their owners, and do so regularly. Unfortunately, this process usually works in just the one direction. Two-way intuitive communication from human to dog and vice versa occurs only when there is a close bond between the two, and the human is prepared to work at developing the intuitive side of his or her nature.

There are many reasons why two-way intuitive communication is so rare. The most common reason is that the human owners do not expect their dog to possess psychic abilities. Consequently, they ignore any indications to the contrary, and their dogs use their intuition at a level that provides enough necessary information without attracting attention. Occasionally, a dog will persist until it gradually educates the humans in its life, but this is rare. Only a few owners expect their dog to possess psychic ability. These people encourage and stimulate their pet's sixth sense, enhancing and enriching the relationship.

Another reason why psychic communication is rare is that many people want a dog to conform to their own expectations. They do not want a psychic dog. They want a "normal" dog. Of course, they do not realize that a normal dog *is* a psychic dog.

Dogs possess considerable precognitive abilities as well. There are many documented accounts of dogs who know in advance when their humans are going to have an epileptic attack. In the early 1990s, an English veterinarian, Andrew Edney, conducted the first study of this phenomenon. He found that the age, sex, and breed of dog made no difference. However, they all became anxious and did whatever was needed to help. This included leading the person to a safe place, running for help, or alerting other people to the imminent attack.[21]

Dr. Milan Ryzl reported an intriguing example of precognition. A worker in an explosives factory had a beautiful collie who accompanied him to work each day. One day, the dog walked part of the way to work and refused to go any farther. The worker was so surprised at his dog's behavior that he discussed it with a colleague who happened to walk past. An hour or so later, his wife called him at the factory as the dog had returned home and was behaving strangely. The worker told his wife what had happened. About an hour later there was an explosion in the factory and everyone was killed.[22]

Dogs appear to be extremely aware of ghosts, and there are many accounts throughout history of their reactions. In 1663, for example, a woman in Paris was disturbed late one night when one of the shutters on her bedroom window opened by itself. She heard the sound of rustling silk, but was unable to see anyone. Her dog could, though. He ran around "as if crazed." A couple of days later, this lady heard that her father had been killed at Crécy at the same time (11 P.M.) that she was awakened.[23]

Jed Tompkins, a friend of mine, told me a similar story. He was living in Portland, Oregon, when his father suffered a fatal heart attack in Bristol, England.

"It was five-thirty and I'd had a hard day at work. I was pouring myself a stiff Scotch when I felt a sudden breeze. I turned around and saw that the door leading to our patio had opened. That had never happened before. I was about to walk over to close it when I suddenly had a clear impression that my father had died. It was a sudden knowledge that appeared in my mind. I couldn't accept it, though. It was impossible as Dad was in perfect health. I'd taken him to the airport just a week before.

"At the same time I was thinking these thoughts, Margot, our elderly poodle, leapt to her feet and began barking.

It wasn't her normal bark. She seemed terrified and constantly appeared to snap at something that was invisible to me. Margot was old and arthritic. She hadn't leapt to her feet in years, and I couldn't remember her ever being agitated. After a couple of minutes of barking and attempting to attack an invisible presence, she went under the dining room table and whimpered.

"I felt such a strong feeling of concern that I went hunting for Dad's itinerary, so I could phone his hotel in England. While I was looking for it, the phone rang. I knew what I was going to hear before I answered it."

Margot was obviously able to see the spectral presence of Jed's father.

"I was confused at the time," Jed told me. "But now it gives me a sense of peace to know that Dad came back to say goodbye."

While working on this book I asked people everywhere I went if their pets were psychic. Many people thought I was crazy for even thinking about the possibility. Other people took the question seriously, but denied that their pets had ever shown any sign of psychic ability. Others accepted that their pets were psychic, and were happy to relate instances that they had experienced or witnessed.

There have always been disagreements among dog owners as to which type of dog is the most intuitive. Some people claim that poodles are more naturally intuitive than other dogs. Others claim that German shepherds are the most intuitive. Still others vote for the Airedale. I have not had a close association with these breeds of dogs, but have enjoyed loving bonds with Labradors, boxers, basset hounds, and a variety of mongrels. In my experience, all dogs are psychic, and no particular breed can claim more ability than another. The most important factor is that the owner is prepared to establish a psychic bond with his or her pet.

Of course, every dog, like every person, is different. We all possess different natural skills and potentials. Dogs, like all other animals, are as varied as we are. Even two dogs from the same litter can be totally different from each other.

This is why it is impossible to draw up a list of the most intelligent breeds of dogs. It is simply impossible to compare the intelligence of a Shih Tzu with that of a German shepherd, for instance. Dr. Stanley Coren, a psychology professor and author of *The Intelligence of Dogs*, made a list of dogs in order of intelligence. Not surprisingly, this list was greeted with howls of protest from dog owners who claimed that their dogs were supremely intelligent, even though they came near the bottom of Dr. Coren's list. Dr. Coren says that you can increase the intelligence of your dog by simply talking to it. "I don't mean . . . love talk . . . If you say to the dog each time you're going to go out of the house 'Let's go out . . .' or 'Do you want a cookie?' . . . whenever you're going to be giving them a treat . . . after a while the dog is going to learn that those sounds . . . and those wavings of the hand mean something."[24]

A psychic bond, once established, will never fade. As a young man I spent time in Cornwall, England, and established a close bond with my landlady's young basset hound, Lily. This dog had been the runt of the litter and was very nearly put down at birth. When I knew her she was two years old, and was about half the size of most basset hounds of the same age. I loved Cornwall and was sorry to leave, but the hardest part was leaving Lily behind. Ten years later, I returned to Cornwall and paid an unexpected visit to my landlady's house. I had lost contact with the family years before and had no idea if they were still living there. To my surprise, an elderly basset hound stood at the gate waiting for me, exactly as she had done every evening when I lived there. My former landlady knew that an unexpected visitor was due, as Lily had been behaving strangely all morning, repeatedly running to the gate and looking up and down the street. It appeared that Lily knew I was going to be visiting that day.

There are many stories told of the intuitive capabilities of dogs. The problem is that most of them cannot be verified. One well-known story that has been extensively researched concerns an Airedale bitch who saved the lives of her owners during the Second World War. One night, during an air raid, the family was sheltering under a table in the basement of their home. The dog was not happy with this and kept running to and from the door, becoming more and more agitated all the time. Finally, she tried to push them out from under the table. The family reluctantly allowed their pet to escort them to the coal cellar. As soon as she had done this, the house collapsed and the table they were hiding under was totally destroyed.[25]

One famous story from the First World War concerns Prince, a terrier who successfully tracked down his master in another country. In September 1914, James Brown left for France with the 1st North Staffordshire regiment. Prince was upset at being left behind. A few days later he disappeared from his home in Hammersmith in search of his master. He found him just a couple of weeks later in a trench in Armentieres. He had managed to cross the English Channel with another troop of soldiers, and had then searched for his master until he found him. As a reward, Prince was made regimental mascot, and was allowed to stay with his master until the end of the war.[26]

The London *Daily Express* recorded a case of precognition in Austria. Johann Steiner, a police-dog handler, looked out of the window of his house at a thunderstorm over the mountains close to his home near Baldramsdorf. He noticed that his seven-year-old German shepherd, Gundo, was not sheltering in his kennel, but was walking up and down and occasionally pawing the wire fence that surrounded his run. As he watched, Gundo ran at the fence, jumped over the top and raced for the house, entering through a ground-floor window. Johann thought that Gundo was simply scared and wanted to shelter in the house, but Gundo gave every impression of wanting to go outside again. He whimpered at Johann, his parents, and the front door. To humor him, Johann opened the door. Gundo ran outside and barked agitatedly at the mountain that loomed over the house. Johann joined him outside and heard the sound of rocks and broken trees through the storm. He realized that a mudslide had begun high in the mountain and was heading toward his house. Johann, his parents, and Gundo got into his car and drove away. They stopped a few hundred yards down the road, just in time to see their house engulfed by a tidal wave of mud. Gundo had saved them just in time.[27]

Robert Morris related another example of the precognition in dogs in a paper he gave at the 1967 winter meeting of the Foundation for Research on the Nature of Man. A visitor to the Foundation had told him that his younger brother had left home for an extended stay in another town. No one had any idea how long it would be before he returned. The boy's pet dog became extremely upset after he left. He ate little and spent most of his time lying outside the boy's bedroom. Gradually, the dog appeared to recover and life carried on as before. One day, the dog became extremely excited. It pawed on the closed door to the boy's bedroom. It then raced down the stairs and out of the house. It ran as far as the main highway, looking both ways before returning to the house. It did this several times during the day. An hour after the last of these, the boy arrived home, to the amazement of everyone, except the dog.[28]

In the early years of the twentieth century, a fishing boat called the *Jeannie Inglis* was based at Baltasound. The boat had a crew of five, and a Bertrand Russell terrier called Nellie who always accompanied them, no matter how bad the weather. One day, when the boat was about to depart on a trip, Nellie went ashore and could not be found. This turned out to be a wise, precognitive decision, as the boat was lost at sea.[29]

Shortly before the First World War, a "talking dog" named Rolf, from Mannheim, Germany, became internationally famous. Apparently, one day Dr. Paula Moeckel, his mistress, became annoyed at her daughter's inability to do basic mathematics and said, "I bet even Rolf could count better than you! Rolf, what is two plus two?" Rolf, who had been sitting beside them, sat up and tapped four times with his paw on Frau Moeckel's arm. His mistress immediately asked him what five plus five was. Rolf tapped out the number ten. After this remarkable start, Frau Moeckel, the wife of a lawyer, dedicated herself to teaching Rolf. On the first evening, Rolf had shown that he understood numbers up to one hundred. Within a few months Rolf was able to recognize each letter of the alphabet. Even this was not enough for Rolf, and he developed a system of paw signals to represent each letter. Eventually, Rolf and Frau Moeckel went on tour and the dog was examined by leading scientists of the day. Rolf proved that he could think clearly, also. In Genoa, a Professor William Mackenzie asked Rolf what the word "autumn" meant. Rolf immediately replied: "It is time for apples." Rolf also displayed a good sense of humor. When a woman asked Rolf if there was anything she could do for him, Rolf replied: "Wag your tail!"[30]

Rolf's daughter, Lola, was just as gifted as her father. However, it took time for her talents to emerge. Scientists were eager to find out what Rolf's daughter could do, but she disappointed everyone. Even Frau Moeckel could not teach her anything except that two taps of her paw meant "yes" and three taps "no." Ultimately, Lola was given to Henny Kindermann, an amazingly patient animal trainer who ultimately wrote *Lola: or the Thought and Speech of Animals*. Frau Kindermann and Lola developed a close, intuitive bond after she told Lola that it would help all dogs if she was prepared to demonstrate what she could do.

Lola developed a quicker way to answer mathematical questions. She decided that her left paw would represent the tens and her right paw the units. Consequently, if the answer was thirty-five, she would tap three times with her left paw, followed by five taps with her right. Ultimately, Lola was able to solve written mathematical problems. She did this by simply glancing at the sheet of paper before tapping out the correct answer.

Lola could also spell phonetically. At one time she was asked the name of the famous Mannheim dog. Instead of spelling out "Rolf," she spelled "main fadr" (*mein Vater* = my father).[31]

There have been many instances of dogs who can perform complicated mathematics and answer questions. Obviously, Rolf and Lola were exceptional, but it appears that virtually all dogs can do much more than we think. Most dogs have a small vocabulary because we do not spend enough time to teach them much more than "sit," "stay," and "lie down." Dogs who are trained to help disabled people know a minimum of ninety commands.

It is never too late to start. However, the best time to train your dog is when he or she is young. In the wild, the mothers of these dogs would be teaching them survival skills every day. Domesticated puppies are keen to learn and enjoy the mental stimulation, which also helps their psychological and physical development.

The first scientific experiments to test the psychic ability of dogs were carried out in Russia. Mars, an Alsatian, was a famous circus dog who could count and dance. Vladimir M. Bekhterov and Alexander Leontovitch, two Soviet academicians, proposed a scientific test. They gave Mars' trainer, Vladimir Durov, a note containing instructions for a task they wanted Mars to undertake. Durov read the note, and then held Mars' head between the palms of his hands. He stared into the dog's eyes. When he let go, nothing happened. He tried again, and this time, Mars went to a room he had never been in before and looked around. The room contained three tables full of files, papers, and books. Mars stood up on his hind legs to examine the objects on the first table. He repeated this with the second table. On the third table, Mars found what he was looking for. He grabbed the phonebook in his mouth and took it back to Durov. This was exactly what the scientists had written on the note, and Durov had successfully transmitted the instructions to Mars telepathically.[32]

After this promising start, Vladimir Bekhterov devised a series of tests that were specially prepared to eliminate any type of conscious or unconscious cues between the dog and his trainer. He even put up screens between himself and the dogs to eliminate any unconscious cues that his body language might provide. Ultimately Mars and a Scottish terrier called Pikki were able to perform a series of unspoken commands that convinced Bekhterov of the reality of telepathic communication between man and dog.

Vladimir Durov became director of the Zoopsychological Laboratory in Moscow and carried on his telepathy experiments until his death in 1934. His book *Training of Animals* describes his methods of developing telepathic skills in dogs. The most important factor was a close emotional bond between the trainer and the dog. Before every test it was important to attract and hold the dog's attention. Durov usually did this by holding the dog's head in his hands and staring into the dog's eyes. He then telepathically sent the specific actions that he wanted the dog to undertake. He did this by picturing the dog doing the required actions. Each successful test was rewarded with a piece of fresh meat.

Durov was an exceptional trainer, and after his death no one was able to train the dogs to the level that he had. However, research continued in the Soviet Union. In 1942, at the Zooveterinary Institute in Kharkov, an experiment was performed with a mother dog and her puppies. At first, the experimenters got her used to having puppies taken away every now and again. Once she became used to this, and accepted it without complaint, the puppies were taken to a room out of earshot where the puppies experienced pain. At the exact same moment, the mother dog became uneasy, began barking, and looked in the direction of the room her puppies were in.[33]

In the United States there have even been government-funded experiments to determine if dogs are psychic. In 1952, representatives from the army asked Dr. J. B. Rhine if he thought that dogs could locate hidden land mines. Obviously, if dogs could sense them, many lives would be saved. Dr. Rhine agreed to conduct some experiments to see if dogs did possess the necessary clairvoyant skills.

The tests were conducted on a beach north of San Francisco, California. Five wooden boxes were buried in the sand to represent hidden land mines. A dog handler, who had no idea where the boxes were buried, led the dogs across the beach. The dogs were trained to sit down when they felt they had detected one of the boxes.

Two hundred and three tests were conducted over a three-month period, and the dogs successfully located the boxes slightly more than 50 percent of the time. However, the handlers noticed that the dogs achieved better results at the start of each test, and that the accuracy rate declined after a short period of time.

Finally, the Army stopped the tests because the results were not consistent enough. The other problem was that the dogs needed to be accompanied by a handler to successfully locate the mines.[34]

Remi Cadoret of the Parapsychology Laboratory at Duke University studied Chris the Wonder Dog in the late 1950s. Chris, a mongrel, was able to answer questions by pawing the correct number of times at his master's shirtsleeves. Remi Cadoret introduced the dog to Zener cards, a deck of twenty-five cards that were frequently used in psychic experiments. The deck consists of five cards each of five designs (circle, plus sign, square, star, and wavy lines). The cards were placed in black envelopes and thoroughly mixed to ensure that no one knew their correct order. This eliminated the possibility of Chris reading anyone's mind. Chris was able to determine which card was in which envelope clairvoyantly. In one series of tests his results were in "the order of a thousand million to one against chance expectation."[35]

Another scientific test was more conclusive. Aristed Esser, a psychiatrist at Rockland State Hospital in New York, was inspired by rumors that the Soviets had been testing animals for ESP with good results.[36] Dr. Esser decided to find out if dogs responded telepathically when their masters or canine relatives felt threatened in any way.

One of his first experiments was to place two beagles who had been trained as hunting dogs in a room at one end of a hospital. Their master was placed in a room at the other end of the hospital. His task was to fire an airgun at colored slides of animals that were displayed on a wall of the room at random intervals. His dogs began barking and whining as soon as he fired the gun, even though they could neither see nor hear what he was doing.

A later experiment utilized a boxer dog and his mistress. The dog was placed in a soundproof room, with a device that measured his heartbeat. The woman was placed in another room. Suddenly a man charged into this room and began yelling at her. The lady had no idea that this was part of the experiment and was terrified. At the exact moment that this occurred, the heart rate of the boxer in the soundproof room increased dramatically.

Another test involved two boxers, a mother and son. Again, they were placed in separate rooms. When one of the experimenters used a newspaper to threaten the younger dog, the mother dog immediately cowered.

YOUR PSYCHIC DOG

Your dog is likely to be much more intelligent than you think. He or she will enjoy performing psychic experiments, as it will be seen as yet another way of pleasing you. Do not keep practicing these tests for hours on end, as the success rate will decline as your dog tires and loses interest. Twenty minutes is about the right length of time. Regular short sessions are much better than a lengthy session every now and again. Be lavish in your praise every time your dog succeeds in any of these tests.

Be aware that psychic abilities do not develop in a steady fashion. Your dog may start out well, and then appear to lose ground. This is normal. Keep on practicing and further progress will be made.

Most people want to show their dog's skills off to others. Your dog is extremely aware of the thought processes of everyone around him or her. If you try to show your dog's talents to someone who is skeptical, your dog will probably refuse to perform or will perform badly. However, when surrounded by pleasant, open-minded people, your dog will be keen to demonstrate.

Color Test

For years it was thought that dogs could see only black and white. However, it is now known that dogs can see tints of color, similar to light pastel. They can easily recognize a red ball from a blue ball, but have problems similar to people with red-green color blindness and find it hard to determine the colors from greenish yellow to red.[37]

For this test you need six large wooden blocks, each painted a different color. I use the primary colors: red, blue, black, green, yellow, and white. Place these in a row several feet away from you. Show them to your dog, picking them up one at a time and telling him what color each one is. Choose one color, and show this one to your dog several times. Mix the blocks up and place them in a row. Ask your dog to fetch you the block of the color that you had chosen. Once your dog can do this, do the same with the other colors.

Now you can start on the test proper. Mix up the blocks and ask your dog to fetch, say, the blue one. Be lavish with your praise each time he or she is successful. Keep on practicing this until it is obvious that your dog can identify each block by its color.

Up until now, this has been an intelligence test. Your dog will enjoy fetching the correct colors for you, and will consider this experiment to be a wonderful game. In fact, you can expand the game even more. You can ask your dog to fetch the block that matches the colors that you are wearing. You can ask your dog to bring you his or her favorite, or least-liked, color. You will find that these choices remain constant. Now it is time to turn this game into a telepathy test.

Mentally decide on a color and send a telepathic message to your dog, asking him or her to bring that particular block to you. Focus your thoughts on your dog walking over, choosing the specific block, and bringing it back to you. Your dog may seem puzzled or perplexed at first, as he or she will be used to you asking for them out loud. However, after a possible slight resistance to begin with, your dog will fetch the color that you are thinking about.

Naturally, this test can be performed with any group of objects that your dog can pick up and bring to you.

Time for a Walk? Test

This is another test in telepathy. Sit down somewhere in a different room to your dog. Close your eyes and think about taking your dog for a walk. Picture yourself making the usual preparations and then stepping out of the house and starting the walk. Visualize your dog and what he or she would normally be doing at the start of a walk.

It is likely that your dog will be standing excitedly in front of you, ready for a walk, before you have finished thinking about it. Of course, this test should be done at a time when you do not normally go for a walk. Reward your dog by taking him or her for a walk.

This test can also be done for anything else your dog likes to do. It also works in reverse. Whenever I thought about giving our dog a bath, he would disappear (see "Bath-Time Test").

A Side Visit Test

While taking your dog for a walk, think about a place on the route that you would like to visit. It needs to be somewhere that you do not stop at regularly. If your walk takes you past a friend's house, for instance, think how nice it would be to visit him or her. See if your dog leads the way into your friend's home without any verbal or physical cues from you.

What Would You Like to Do? Test

This is a more advanced test. Sit down quietly somewhere, close your eyes, and send your dog a psychic message asking what he or she would like to do.

You may find that your dog immediately appears, excited that you are going to do what he or she wants. At the same time, you may receive a clear mental impression as to what it is he or she wants to do. If the mental impression does not come through, follow your pet and see if that provides enough clues for you to carry out the desired response.

Bruce, our Labrador, usually wanted to go out in the car. Sometimes he would ask for a game with his ball. Occasionally, he would decide on a walk, but most of the time, a request for a ride in the car would come to me. He always sat on the back seat, looking from side to side, making the most of the journey.

Multiple Request Test

This fascinating test involves mentally suggesting that your dog does a number of actions. You might, for instance, suggest that he or she go to the bedroom and fetch your slippers before picking up a plaything so that the two of you can have a game.

I find this works best if the dog is sleeping and the tasks are pleasant ones. Sit down in the same room as your dog and think about the actions you want him or her to perform. Think about each action in turn, saying mentally to yourself something like this: "I want you to fetch my slippers first, and then go and find your rubber banana so that we can have a game."

When you first experiment with this, you may have to think of the first task until your dog has done it, and then think of the second task until it has been successfully performed, before going on to the third. However, in time, you will be able to think of a whole series of activities and your dog will faithfully do them all in order.

The Find It Test

If your dog has a well-loved toy, you will be able to conduct this experiment. When your dog is out of the room, hide the toy in a place where he or she will be able to find it. Call the dog to you and ask it to find the object.

If the toy has a place where it is usually kept, your dog will go there first. It will probably be reluctant to look anywhere else. Think about where you have hidden the toy, and try to send these thoughts to your dog. Telepathically, lead it to the object step by step.

Do not repeat this exercise more than once a day. When your dog finds the object, spend some time with your pet enjoying a game with the object.

Obviously, well-loved toys develop an odor that can be picked up by our pets. To avoid this, try placing the objects in airtight containers, and see if your pet is still able to locate the toy. I find that plastic kitchenware works well. This partially replicates tests done with cats at Duke University in Durham, North Carolina, in which cat food was hidden in identical sealed containers, eliminating the senses of sight and smell. The researchers at Durham felt that the results of this test "make clairvoyance in cats the most likely explanation."[38]

Clairvoyancy Test

This is a variation of the previous test. You will need five or six identical boxes. Place the toy inside one of them. Place other items in the other boxes. Close the boxes, mix them up, and then ask your dog to find the box that contains his or her toy.

Bath-Time Test

Our dog, Bruce, hated having a bath and always disappeared as soon as we even thought about it. He always responded to a call, except when it was bath-time. If your dog hates a specific activity, you can try the following test in telepathy.

Your dog must be out of sight. Sit down, close your eyes, and think about the task that your dog detests. With Bruce, I would think about giving him a bath. Think about it for at least five minutes. Then call your dog and see if he or she comes. Your dog may do as Bruce did, and simply not respond at all. Alternatively, he or she may respond but come up to you looking distinctly unhappy. This is a success, also, as your dog obviously read your thoughts. The experiment is considered a failure if your dog bounds up to you in his or her normal fashion.

*There is no secret so close
as that between a rider and his horse.*
—R. S. SURTEES (1805–1864)

4

The Noble Horse

It would be hard to find an animal that is more admired or valued than the horse. They have served humankind for some five to six thousand years. There are numerous cave drawings that depict scenes involving horses. Primitive people were dependent on horses. They hunted them for food before learning how to tame them to gain increased mobility. Since then they have been ridden into battle, used to haul heavy loads, and been exploited in many other ways. Yet they have also been loved and cherished by people who valued their friendship, noble spirit, stamina and beauty.

When El Cid, the legendary Spanish warrior, was offered a horse by his godfather, he chose a scrawny, white, awkward colt, even though there were several much finer-looking horses he could have chosen. His godfather thought El Cid had made a foolish choice and named the horse Babieca, which means "a fool." However, El Cid loved his horse, trained him with care, and ultimately proved his godfather wrong. When El Cid became leader of the Spanish army, Babieca carried him into every battle. Unfortunately, in his last great battle, El Cid was mortally wounded. Before dying, he asked his men to secretly embalm him so that Babieca could carry him into battle one last time. El Cid's men were demoralized and upset at the loss of their leader. When El Cid appeared during the battle, his men could not believe their eyes. They regained their lost momentum and soundly defeated the Moors.[1]

The Roman emperor Caligula made his favorite horse a senator. Incitatus (which means "fast speeding") won every race he participated in. The grateful Caligula gave him a beautiful villa, with plenty of slaves to look after him. Incitatus had a marble bedroom with straw that was changed every day. His drinking trough was pure gold. Incitatus was even invited to Caligula's wild parties and ate the same food as the other guests.[2]

Horses have played a major role in human history, but today it is rare for city dwellers to even see a horse. Occasionally, mounted police are used for crowd control, and create a striking impression. Fortunately, horseracing and equestrian events on television enable people to observe horses in competition. The close bond between a horse and his or her rider, particularly in equestrian events, is clearly obvious.

Horses are highly intelligent animals with senses that far exceed our own. They are totally attuned to their environment. Their strong senses of touch and smell play a major part in establishing relationships with humans and other horses. They use their acute sense of smell to determine any nervousness in their handlers. Professional handlers swear that horses can smell fear in timid riders. Stallions possess such a strong sense of smell that they can sense a mare in heat from half a mile away.[3] Horses dislike the smell of blood, and are obviously unhappy when close to an abattoir.

Their sense of hearing is much stronger than ours, too. We can hear up to twenty thousand cycles a second, but horses can hear up to twenty-five thousand. In both people and horses, this tends to decline with age.

The horse's sense of sight is unusual. Their eyes are larger than those of elephants and whales, and they can see well at night. They focus on objects by raising and lowering their heads. They see less detail than we do, but are much better at detecting movement. Horses are able to move their eyes independently, and the setting of them, on the side of the head, gives them good lateral and almost all around (340 degrees) vision. Horses have blind spots directly ahead and directly behind them. Consequently, it is best not to approach them from these directions as you are likely to startle them.

The psychic perception of horses has been known for thousands of years. Hours before the famous earthquake in San Francisco in 1906, horses became agitated and many broke out of their stalls. Horses in the wild frequently demonstrate psychic ability when they are disturbed. Although some of the horses may be out of sight and sound of the others, at the slightest sign of danger, all of them will become aware of it, first pricking their ears, snorting, and then moving away from the potential danger.

One common example of the psychic ability of horses was related to me by a friend in England who enjoys fox hunting. His horse always knows when they are going hunting and becomes excited, well before my friend arrives at the stables. I have been told many similar stories about the uncanny ability of horses to know in advance about enjoyable activities.

Many years ago, a Spanish carthorse refused to go into a mountain tunnel that she had happily passed through many times before. Her driver became frustrated and angry, particularly when a line of angry riders built up behind them. The mare was demonstrating her precognitive gifts. Shortly afterward, the tunnel collapsed.[4]

There are many accounts of horses refusing to go anywhere near haunted places. They have a highly developed sense of impending danger, and appear to intuitively understand the moods of their handlers.

In her classic novel *Black Beauty*, Anna Sewell had Black Beauty refuse to cross a bridge in the dark, even when whipped by his master. The bridge had been broken in the middle by a storm, and Black Beauty intuitively knew this.[5]

In his book *Animal Folklore, Myth and Legend*, Anthony Wootton tells of a farmer who always knew when to put the kettle on. His mare's foal would become excited about half an hour before his mother returned from the market, neighing loudly and hitting the door of his stable. As the trip to the market and back varied enormously in time, the foal was obviously picking up his mother's thoughts telepathically.[6]

This strong intuitive understanding is put to good use in the international Riding for the Disabled Association programs. My sister, Penny, assisted at one such program for many years and could never get over the incredible empathy the horses had for people with physical and mental problems. Penny worked with children suffering from Down's syndrome, and frequently talked of the close bonds that developed between the horses and these children.

Horses communicate using all of their senses. Sound is important, of course, but horses do not have a large range of sounds to choose from. The soft whicker that mares use to reassure their foals is unmistakable, and is also sometimes heard when the horse thinks food is coming. Horses whinny with excitement, snort when something unusual attracts their attention, and squeal or grunt when being aggressive. They also whinny when a horse has become separated from the group, or if they see one of their companions in the distance.

However, communication involves a variety of other physical signals such as mutual grooming, body language, and smell. Mutual grooming involves taste, touch, and smell, and is done when making friends with other horses or to show friendship. Stroking and patting by humans also helps create close bonds. Horses blow into each other's nostrils and, partly thanks to *The Horse Whisperer*, many people have learned that this is an excellent way of making friends with a horse.

There are an increasing number of horse psychics who are able to tune in to individual horses and tell you about them. The most famous of these was a retired sailor called Fred Kimball who died in 1996 at the age of ninety-one. People would phone him, and give him the name and sex of their horses. Kimball would then psychically tune in to the horse and have a mental conversation with him or her. After this, Kimball was able to tell his clients about their horse's psychological or physical ailments. Kimball charged twenty-five dollars, and relied on people's honesty in posting a check to him.[7]

The body language of horses is easy to read. If a horse turns its quarters to you when you enter its stall, for instance, you need to proceed with caution. Shaking of the head, swishing of the tail, and stamping a hind leg all send out messages of irritation.

The bearing of the horse shows how positive and excited he or she is. When the horse feels good about itself, it holds itself regally and looks impressive. When it is tired or dispirited, its whole bearing droops, and the horse appears smaller.

Their ears are controlled by thirteen sets of muscles and are seldom still. They are incredibly mobile, and receive sound signals as well as reveal the horse's moods, feelings, and emotional state. When they are pricked strongly forward, it is a sign that the horse is interested in something and is paying little attention to the rider. The ears become stiffly erect when something appears worrying or unusual. The ears are lowered and become flaccid when the horse is relaxed or tired. They can even flop loosely when the horse is in pain or exhausted. It is a sign of aggression, displeasure, or anger if they are laid hard back and flattened against the head. When the ears are twitching and mobile, the horse is being attentive to the task at hand. If the horse is fearful of the rider, the ears will be stuck out sideways, with the openings facing toward the rider.

The tail is an accurate gauge of the horse's feelings, also. When it is held high, the horse is feeling excited, alert, and exuberant. When the tail droops, the horse is submissive, fearful, stressed, tired, or in pain. Sometimes, the tail can be held so high that it flicks over the horse's back. This is commonly found when a young horse is trying to encourage another horse to play. Horses swish their tails when they are annoyed or frustrated. The power of the switch increases when the horse is angry. It is a sign of increased anger (and the possibility of a kick) when the tail is flicked high in the air and then down with great force.

Horses are highly intelligent animals with excellent memories. They quickly learn to discriminate between designs. In a test involving twenty pairs of designs, horses were able to tell them apart with ease, and retained the memories of nineteen of them twelve months later.[8]

People who work closely with horses often develop a psychic connection with them. In his book *Talking with Horses*, Henry Blake gives several instances of psychic communication between himself and the horses he was training. He also observed a number of occasions when his horses were able to communicate telepathically with other horses. If one horse was frightened, for instance, other horses would clearly respond even when they were far away.[9]

There have been a number of horses over the years who appeared to perform complicated mathematical feats. In the early part of the twentieth century Clever Hans, from Elberfeld, Germany, was the best known of these. He was able to perform mathematical calculations by tapping a hoof on the ground. He would answer other questions by shaking or nodding his head. If he was asked what three times two was, he would tap the ground six times.

His owner, Wilhelm von Osten, who had formerly been a mathematics teacher, claimed that he was not cueing Hans in any way. He also never tried to make any money from Clever Hans' abilities. People were amazed at Clever Hans' abilities and it was said that he had the mental capabilities of an eight-year-old human. Even the kaiser became interested, and appointed a commission to examine this phenomenon.

Before he died in 1909, von Osten asked a friend to become his partner. He taught Karl Krall everything he knew about horse training. Krall used the same techniques on four other horses: Muhamed, Zarif, Berto, and Hänschen. They, along with Hans, became famous as the Elberfeld Horses. Karl Krall found that the four new horses were able to learn extremely quickly. He devised a special chart for them that consisted of forty-nine squares, depicting all the letters and diphthongs in the German language. This enabled the horses to "speak" by tapping a hoof on the appropriate squares.

However, two investigators, Professor C. Stumpf and Otto Pfungst, found that Clever Hans was unable to answer a question if the questioner did not already know the answer. This meant that Clever Hans was actually reading cues from his audience. When Clever Hans was asked a question, his audience would naturally look at his hooves. When he reached the correct answer, the audience would look at his face again, and Hans would stop tapping the ground. Hans had somehow accidentally learned a clever trick. Clever Hans was also able to detect the increased tension in his audience as the tapping came close to the correct answer. People were concerned that he might make a mistake, and Hans was able to read this and stop at the correct time.

Hans certainly deserved to be called "Clever Hans," but for his feats of observation and ability at reading body language, rather than for his mathematical skill.[10] Since then, animal behaviorists have had to be extremely careful not to fall into this trap when investigating animal intelligence. In fact, this occurrence has become known as the "Clever Hans phenomenon."

The scientists of the day were relieved to find a rational explanation for Clever Hans' abilities, but it seems that they may have stopped investigating too soon. Maurice Maeterlinck, the Belgian writer who received the Nobel Peace Prize for Literature in 1911, investigated the Elberfeld horses. He was determined to devise tests that could not be answered by unconscious sensory clues. On one occasion, he was alone with Muhamed, experimenting with different words that came to his mind. He thought of the name of the hotel he was staying in (Weiderhof), and Muhamed spelled "Weiderhoz." Karl Krall, the trainer, came in and told the horse that the word had been misspelled. Muhamed immediately changed the final letter to *f.*

Maeterlinck devised a test in clairvoyance. He took three cards, each with a number printed on it, mixed them, and then placed them facedown on the ground in front of Muhamed. No one knew what number the three cards created, but Muhamed immediately tapped out the correct answer. Maeterlinck conducted the same test with the other horses, and they were successful every time. Obviously, in this instance, the horses were not picking up sensory cues from anyone.[11]

Black Bear was another horse who showed a talent for mathematics. However, he also appeared to have clairvoyant capabilities. According to a report in the April 1931 issue of *Psychic Research*, Black Bear was able to look at the back of playing cards and determine which suits and denominations they were. If he did not know the answer, Black Bear would refuse to guess. On one occasion, a woman named Mrs. Fletcher came to see him. Mr. Barett, Black Bear's trainer, asked the horse if an anniversary was about to be celebrated. Black Bear immediately spelled out "birthday," which was correct. Mrs. Fletcher then asked when it would be. Black Bear replied, "Friday." "What date will that be?" Mrs. Fletcher inquired. "August 3." This was the date of Mrs. Fletcher's birthday, and she was the only person present who knew that. Obviously, Black Bear was gaining that information telepathically or clairvoyantly from Mrs. Fletcher's mind.[12]

In 1929, Professor J. B. Rhine published his first paper in the field of parapsychology.[13] This concerned another horse, Lady Wonder, who was also able to answer questions. Lady Wonder's owner, Mrs. Claudia Fonda, first realized that her horse had psychic abilities when the filly cantered up to her while she was thinking about going for a ride. Thinking that this was a coincidence, Mrs. Fonda tried again on different occasions. Lady Wonder responded far too frequently for it to simply be a matter of chance. Mrs. Fonda contacted Professor Rhine, who had recently come to Duke University. Instead of using her hooves to answer questions, Lady Wonder pointed her nose toward letters and numbers printed on a board. Thinking that the horse might be obtaining unconscious cues from her mistress, the researchers asked Mrs. Fonda to absent herself from the tests. This made no difference.[14]

Lady Wonder achieved some incredible successes. Someone asked her about a boy named Danny Matson who had been missing for several months. Lady Wonder spelled out "Pittsfield." The police immediately began searching in the Pittsfield, Massachusetts, area, without success. A police captain realized that an abandoned quarry nearby was known as the Field and Wilde Water Pit. The police searched the quarry and found the boy's body.[15]

Lady Wonder was also precognitive. One day she spelled out the word "engine." This was a totally new word for her. Shortly afterward, a tractor came down the road. She also predicted that the United States and Russia would take part in the Second World War, and successfully predicted that Harry Truman would win the 1948 election when almost every commentator had predicted that he would lose. Lady also developed a talent for predicting the winners of horse races. However, once magazines began publishing articles about her abilities in this area, racing officials asked her to stop.

In 1932, a newspaper reporter asked Lady Wonder who would be nominated by the Democratic Party for the upcoming presidential elections. Lady Wonder spelled out "ROO," and then paused. When she started again, she spelled out "I can't spell the name." At the end of 1932, Franklin Delano Roosevelt became president of the United States.[16]

Professor Rhine concluded that Lady Wonder had telepathic abilities. Mrs. Fonda agreed with this. She also thought that every horse was capable of doing the feats that Lady did, provided the owner was interested enough to teach his or her horse using a chart of the alphabet. The Fondas were not interested in making money from their talented horse and turned down many offers from Hollywood. They did nothing to publicize or promote Lady, and never got used to the crowds of people who visited Lady every day. The Fondas were Christian people who believed that Lady's abilities came from God. However, Mrs. Fonda felt that if people had problems they should ask God for help, rather than consult a horse. Lady Wonder had a heart attack and died on March 19, 1957, at the advanced age of thirty-three years.[17]

Roy Rogers told everyone that Trigger was "the smartest horse in the movies." Trigger, a beautiful palomino, starred in eighty-seven movies, most of them with Roy Rogers. He knew more than sixty tricks, such as walking 150 yards on his hind legs, taking a gun out of a holster with his mouth, and drinking milk out of a bottle. He knew the numbers from one to twenty, and was able to add and subtract in the same way that the Elberfield horses did.[18]

No doubt because of the popularity of horse racing, many people have precognitive dreams about horse races. Not all of these have to do with picking potential winners. In the *Proceedings* of the British Society for Psychic Research is recorded the dream of an Irish jockey who was due to ride a horse called Phoenicia at the Manchester Race Course on the following day. In his dream he saw that he did not ride the horse, but that it had won the race with another jockey. He also dreamed that his father, back home in Ireland, saw "from the evening paper that Phoenicia had won without me in the saddle." As he was getting ready for the race on the following day, the jockey was handed a telegram from the horse's owner telling him that another jockey was to take his place. Phoenicia won the race. The jockey's dream also intimated that his father had complained angrily to the owner of the horse because he had not let his son ride. This also occurred, and the owner later apologized to the jockey for replacing him at the last moment.[19]

YOUR PSYCHIC HORSE

Because horses are extremely intelligent and alert to all sorts of subconscious cues, it is not easy to create tests to determine their psychic abilities. Here are some tests that have stood the test of time.

Telepathy Test

This is the test that first alerted Mrs. Fonda to Lady Wonder's psychic abilities. Stand somewhere close to your horse, but preferably out of sight. Think about your horse and see if he or she responds by coming over to you.

If you have no success with this, try this experiment again by standing in a position where your horse can see you. Once he or she responds regularly to your thoughts, place yourself out of sight and see if the same thing occurs.

Your belief in the success of this experiment is vital. Horses are highly intuitive, and your horse will immediately sense any feelings of disappointment you may have if the test does not work right away. Likewise, your horse will instantly pick up any skepticism you may have.

For this experiment you will need two squares or circles made of cardboard or plywood. They should be approximately two feet in diameter. Paint one of them yellow and the other blue.

Until recently, it was thought that horses could not see color. However, an interesting experiment demonstrated that they do. Two horses were tested by being led into a room containing several mangers, all containing oats. In front of one manger was a colored card. The other mangers had cards that were in various shades of gray. The horses were allowed to eat only from the manger that was indicated by the colored card. Every day, the color was changed and all the cards changed position. The horses quickly learned that they had to go to the manger containing the colored card if they wanted to be fed. Horses have a much weaker sense of color than we do, and respond best to yellows and greens, followed by blues. They respond least of all to reds.[20]

Show your colored circles to your horse before placing them on the ground directly in front of your horse's front hooves. Your horse may feel nervous about this initially, and may tentatively touch them with his or her hooves.

Tell your horse that you are conducting an experiment, and that the circle in front of his or her right foot represents the answer "yes" while the other one represents "no." If the answer is "yes," you want your horse to tap the circle with his or her right hoof, and to use the left hoof if the answer is "no."

Repeat these instructions several times while gently stroking or caressing your horse. Finally, ask if he or she understands. Your horse may, or may not, respond the first time you try this.

If you get a positive response, continue with questions that can be answered with a "yes" or "no." You should consider it a positive response if your horse taps "no" in answer to your question. Your horse is responding to your question, but is unsure what you are attempting to do. Simply explain everything again. Tell your horse that you love him or her, and are conducting these experiments so that the two of you can establish an even closer bond.

No response at all means that your horse has no idea what you are trying to do. Explain again and see if your horse answers. Remain confident and positive. Remove the circles and bring them out again on the following day. Keep doing this until your horse understands what you are trying to do.

Once communication has been established in this way, there is no limit to the number of questions you can ask. However, do not overtire your horse by plying him or her with questions for hours on end. Twenty minutes is the maximum time you should allow for question answering, unless your horse is obviously enjoying the experience. You can always ask your horse if he has had enough, and continue or finish according to the reply.

Some horses respond to this test extremely well and enjoy it. If your horse is like this, you can continue with the experiment by teaching him or her numbers and the letters of the alphabet to widen the range of the questions and answers.

So far, this experiment has been a test of your horse's ability at understanding and answering your spoken questions. Once your horse has become used to this experiment, you will find that you do not need to say the questions out loud. You can think about your questions and your horse will answer, either with a "yes" or "no" response, or by sending a thought into your mind.

Mind-to-Mind Communication

If you are close to your horse, you probably already do this unconsciously. While grooming your horse, think gently about him or her. Allow your mind to be as still and receptive as possible. Send thoughts of love to your horse.

After several minutes of this, mentally ask your horse if he or she loves you. Wait and see if a reply appears in your mind. Once you receive an answer, you can continue communicating by exchanging thoughts.

More information on communicating in this way is included in the next chapter.

Right or Left Test

This is a test that was devised by Harry Blake and included in his book *Talking with Horses: A Study of Communication Between Man and Horse.*

Harry placed two food buckets ten yards apart. One of the buckets was empty, while the other contained the horse's breakfast. He telepathically told his horse, Cork Beg, which bucket to go to. It took a few days before the horse consistently went to the bucket he wanted him to go to. Harry Blake then began a more advanced test. Both buckets contained food and Harry thought about the bucket he wanted Cork Beg to eat from. For the first five days, he alternated the bucket he thought about. Then he concentrated on the left-hand bucket for four days in a row. Finally, on the tenth day, he focused on the right-hand bucket and Cork Beg went directly to it. He then continued with the experiment by varying the container he thought about.[21]

Me Too Test

This is another test devised by Harry Blake. He believes that horses communicate with each other telepathically and devised this test to confirm this hypothesis. You will need two horses that are close to each other, either as companions or with a strong blood connection.

Separate the horses, so that they can no longer see or hear each other. Feed one of them and see what reaction the other horse gives. In twenty-one times out of twenty-four tests, Harry Blake found that the other horse became excited and demanded to be fed, even though it was not the regular feeding time.[22]

Jealousy Test

You will need two horses who are close to each other to attempt this test. When they are out of sight and sound of each other, make a fuss over one of the horses. Shortly, the other horse will show signs of anger or jealousy, as he or she is being left out.

All animals are equal
but some animals are more equal than others.
—GEORGE ORWELL (1903–1950)

5

Animals Tall and Small

In this book I have concentrated on cats, dogs, and horses. This is because these are the most popular pets, and the ones who are most likely to engage in psychic communication with their owners. However, there is almost no limit to the variety of animal pets that people have. I have known people who have kept axolotls, crickets, praying mantises, spiders, salamanders, frogs, lizards, snakes, turtles, and chimpanzees. A good friend of mine keeps and breeds vultures, as they are becoming an endangered species. Over the years, in addition to cats, dogs, and a horse, I have kept bees, rabbits, guinea pigs, frogs, lizards, turtles, and a tortoise.

No matter what sort of animal your pet is, you will be able to establish a psychic connection with him or her.

J. Allen Boone, author of *Kinship with All Life*, was able to communicate telepathically with a pet fly.[1]

All animals appear to have a psychic sense. In Japan, goldfish are used to provide advance warning of earthquakes and avalanches. Their frantic movements through the water alert people to the imminent danger. Animals in zoos also frequently give warning of impending danger.

The sacred geese on Capitoline Hill in Rome were a good example of this. According to Plutarch, in 390 B.C.E., the geese began cackling excitedly to give warning that the Gauls were about to attack.

In 1944, a duck in Freiberg, Germany, began quacking incessantly shortly before an Allied air raid. The sirens had not gone off, but all the same, many of the inhabitants heeded the duck's warning and ran to the air-raid shelters. They survived the attack, and after the war erected a statue in honor of the duck who had saved their lives.[2]

Late in the afternoon of August 17, 1959, thousands of birds that had made their home on Lake Hegben in Montana flew away. Several hours later, the region was rocked by several major earthquakes, and the Hegben Dam cracked, releasing a deluge of water. Many people were killed, but the rangers found no dead animals. Like the birds, they had left the scene many hours beforehand.[3]

Pierre Duval and Evelyn Montredon are the pseudonyms of two biologists in France who tested mice for precognition. Sadly, these two scientists felt unable to publish their findings under their own names at the time. It is now known that their real names are J. Meyer and R. Chauvin.

A mouse was placed in a box, which was divided in two by a barrier that the mouse could jump over. An electric shock that lasted five seconds was sent once a minute to one side of the box or the other. Which side was to be shocked at any time was determined by a random number generator. This eliminated the possibility that the mouse was reading the thoughts of the scientists conducting the experiment. Naturally, the point of the experiment was to see if the mouse could predict which side of the box the shock would occur in, and jump to the other side.

The results were amazing. The scientists ignored all the times where the mouse simply stayed where it was, or jumped the barrier after receiving a shock. However, in all the instances where the mouse jumped the barrier before a shock occurred it beat the level of chance by odds of one thousand to one.[4]

Similar results were also obtained in tests conducted at the Institute for Parapsychology in Durham, North Carolina, in 1971. These researchers conducted many more tests than the French had, and experimented with both mice and gerbils.[5]

John Randall researched precognition in mice, rats, and gerbils and came to the conclusion that their ability to foretell the future had "been established beyond all reasonable doubt."[6]

One of the cases that fascinated Dr. J. B. Rhine involved a young boy called Hugh Perkins, from West Virginia, and his pet pigeon. This pigeon had an identifying band around one leg when it arrived in Hugh's backyard. It showed no signs of wanting to leave, and Hugh began feeding it. Over the next twelve months a deep and close bond developed between the pigeon and the boy.

When Hugh suddenly became ill, he was rushed to a hospital one hundred and twenty miles from home, where he had an operation. The following night, there was a gentle tapping at the window of Hugh's room. Hugh could see a pigeon standing on the window ledge, but was not well enough to get out of bed to let him in. The bird had to stay on the ledge all night in the winter snow, until a nurse opened the window in the morning.

Dr. Rhine was puzzled as to how this pigeon had managed to fly one hundred and twenty miles over a mountain range and go to the exact room where his young friend was lying ill in bed.[7]

Scientists have even tested the psychic abilities of fish. Dr. Robert Morris, an animal behaviorist, placed three goldfish in a tank and had an assistant observe which fish appeared to be the most agitated. Dr. Morris then caught one of the fish in a net. The fish he removed was a random choice, but most of the time it was the same fish that the assistant had classed as being agitated. It would appear that the fish had become distressed knowing that it would shortly be caught.[8]

Experiment with your pet by sending him or her telepathic thoughts. Tell your pet how much he or she means to you. Express your appreciation and love. After telling your pet everything you wish to say, sit quietly and see what comes into your mind. You may find your pet sending similar thoughts back to you. You may receive a message, or simply a comforting feeling of reciprocated love.

If you do this on a regular basis you will find your relationship becoming closer and closer. You will be able to exchange thoughts and ideas that will enhance your relationship in many different ways.

This may sound ridiculous until you try it. At one stage I had a pet frog, and was certain that he saw me only as a source of flies to eat. However, every time I communicated telepathically with him, he came and sat by my right hand. He would remain motionless until our telepathic conversation was over and then jump back into the pond. After doing this for a few days, I noticed that he appeared to be waiting for me, and as soon as I sat down beside the pond he came to join me. He was obviously looking forward to our conversation as much as I was.

With practice, there is no limit as to how far you can go. Be patient, and do not try to progress too quickly. Take your time, and enjoy the special bond that will develop as the two of you engage in psychic conversation.

But ask now the beasts, and they shall teach thee;
and the fowls of the air, and they shall tell thee;
Or speak to the earth, and it shall teach thee;
and the fishes of the sea shall declare unto thee;
Who knoweth not in all these
that the hand of the Lord hath wrought this?
In whose hand is the soul of every living thing,
and the breath of all mankind.
—*The Book of Job, 12:7–10*

6

Communicating with Your Pet

I still remember my mother's embarrassment when she discovered a stranger watching her talk to a neighbor's cat. However, she should not have felt embarrassed. We should all talk to our pets as much as possible. This doesn't mean simply saying "pretty puss." You should speak to your pets in the same way you would speak to another person. Tell them what you are doing, and why. Tell them what is going on in your life. Tell them your hopes and dreams. Talk to them about politics, religion, and anything that is going on in your life. The very worst thing that can happen is that you'll establish a closer relationship with your pet, and be happier, healthier, and emotionally more stable, too.

Talk to your pets as equals. Talk to them the way you would talk to any other close friend. You must not talk at or down to your pets. You must also be ready to receive what they say to you. If you have not done this before, you will be amazed at how much your pets know and understand.

Obviously, your pet's view of reality is totally different to yours. Consequently, you need to pay close attention to his or her methods of communication before attempting to transmit and receive messages that both of you will understand.

You can be certain that your pet is an expert at reading and understanding your methods of communication. Some people are naturally good at interspecies communication, but it is a skill that anyone can develop. After all, most pet owners know when their pet is feeling happy, scared, bored, or not feeling well.

Experts in body language tell us that between 75 and 90 percent of all human communication is done nonverbally and below our conscious levels of awareness.[1] Consequently, it should not surprise anyone to discover that they can communicate effectively with their pets using the language of the heart.

The most important single factor in communicating with your pet is love. With strong bonds of love on both sides, success is guaranteed. There is a bonus as well. No matter how many mistakes you make along the way, your pet will forgive you and remain eager to bring the two of you even closer together.

St. Francis of Assisi regularly conversed with animals. Longfellow wrote that Hiawatha learned "of every beast its language." You can do exactly the same.

Your pet probably understands many words. Obviously, he or she will know its name. Your pet will also understand words that relate to its needs, such as "walk," "dinner," and "bedtime." However, your pet knows a great deal more than this.

In the 1850s, in the high country of New Zealand, a plague of sheep rustling occurred. No one knew how it was done, and it took more than two years to find the thief, a Scotsman named James McKenzie. He was a loner who enjoyed exploring the high country in this remote part of the world. One day he discovered a secret valley that was sheltered, contained an abundance of grass, and was well below the snow line. The valley was large enough to secretly conceal a thousand sheep. This gave McKenzie an idea. If he could steal sheep from the Canterbury Plains, hide them in the valley for a while, and then sell them in the markets of Otago, he could make a fortune. Fortunately for him, he had a highly intelligent sheep dog who made the scheme possible.

McKenzie and his dog would visit a sheep station and have a chat with the shepherd. While there, McKenzie would speak to his dog in Gaelic, telling her to return to the spot that night and shepherd the entire flock through a secret pass to the hidden valley. McKenzie and his dog had practiced this many times with his own sheep, and the dog had no difficulty in doing it at night with any flock that McKenzie indicated. Naturally, McKenzie became a suspect. However, it appeared impossible for him to be involved as he was still close to the scene when the crimes were discovered, and he always joined the search parties.

Ultimately, McKenzie was caught and sentenced to five years in prison. He tearfully appealed to the judge for his dog to be imprisoned with him, but this was refused. Many people tried to use the dog as a sheepdog, but without success. However, her puppies were well sought after. Despite the different spelling, James McKenzie gave his name to the Mackenzie Country in the South Island of New Zealand, where he and his dog are still well remembered.[2]

James McKenzie obviously had an exceptionally close bond with his sheep dog, who was able to understand the instructions he gave her and could then carry them out several hours later on her own.

Many years ago, a parrot at the Institut de Psychologie Zoologique in Paris was taught to say the word "cupboard," because that was where his hempseed was kept. The person who fed him had to climb a ladder to reach the food, and the parrot was taught the words "ladder" and "climb." One day, as a test, the parrot's food was placed on a high shelf and the ladder was taken away. When the person came to feed him in the normal way, the parrot called out "cupboard." The man went to the cupboard, which contained millet, and gave this to the parrot. The bird did not enjoy millet and kept biting at the bars of his cage in fury. He called out "cupboard!" all day long. On the second morning, the parrot started to get angry again, but paused to think. When he called out "ladder, climb, cupboard," he was given his hempseed. This parrot not only understood what these words meant, but was also able to think about them and frame them in the right way to get what he wanted.[3]

This parrot was taught to understand and communicate using human words. However, if the person who was feeding him had been prepared to listen, the parrot would have passed on the message telepathically.

Every time you say or think something, you are creating a picture of it in your mind. If you are at all close to your pet, he or she will be able to read those messages and respond to them. That is why your pet frequently knows exactly what you are going to do at the same time that it occurs to you.

We have a pet rabbit called Tibbar ("rabbit" spelled backward). Rabbits are extremely territorial and Tibbar will occasionally bite people when they are foolish enough to put their fingers in his cage. The only two members of the family who have not been bitten are my four-year-old granddaughter, Eden, and I.

Tibbar and I have an extremely close relationship. For many years I performed a magic act and Tibbar and I did hundreds of shows together. He sat in a cage resting on the seat beside me as I drove to and from these shows. One day Tibbar told me that he would prefer to sit on the seat, rather than remain in the cage. Naturally, he did not speak the words, but the idea suddenly came into my mind. I was a bit dubious about this, as I did not want a rabbit moving around in the car and possibly distracting me while I was driving. No sooner had I thought this than Tibbar informed me that he would sit quietly on the seat. I stopped the car, took him out of his cage, and placed him on the seat. We drove the remaining few miles home with Tibbar sitting comfortably on the seat, giving every appearance of enjoying the ride. Tibbar puts up with the magic shows, but adores going for rides in the car. He has never let me down in the several years since he told me that he wanted to sit on the seat beside me. He will occasionally move around on the seat, but has never moved off it while I have been driving.

Eden has known Tibbar all her life. She regularly brings him inside to play with her. She treats him like a friend and talks to him constantly. Tibbar thrives on this attention and appears to enjoy being dressed in doll's clothes and taken for walks in a baby carriage. However, as soon as Eden decides that it is time for Tibbar to go outside again, he will hide under her bed and not let her catch him. He does this as soon as the thought comes to her mind. There is no need for her to say the words out loud.

Obviously, Tibbar is able to understand and respond to whatever Eden and I are thinking about. I am certain he is able to read the minds of everyone else in the household, also, but because they sometimes consider him to be more of a nuisance than a pet, he does not respond to them in the same way he does to Eden and me. Consequently, he feels free to bite them when they put their fingers in his cage. Effective communication between species requires mutual love and respect.

BODY LANGUAGE

Observing your pet's body language is an important part of communication. For instance, you do not need to be a mind reader to sense the tension when two dogs meet each other for the first time. Their tails and ears rise. They walk stiffly toward each other, and stand head to neck for a while before permitting examination of the groin area. You can easily sense the moment when the tension fades. After this, they might frisk and play for a while, as all dogs love the company of other dogs.

Of course, sometimes the scenario does not go exactly like this, and the two dogs may start to fight. This can be alarming for humans who do not understand what is going on. The dogs are fighting for supremacy and usually neither is hurt. The fight is over as soon as both dogs realize which one is the victor. At this point, the dog who has lost will roll over and expose his throat and stomach to the winner. The victor will stand over the losing dog, bare his fangs and snarl for a while. The two dogs will then forget the fight completely, but will always remember which dog is stronger and more powerful than the other.

The wagging tail of a dog is a good example of body language in action. A wagging tail is the dog equivalent of a smile or laugh. Naturally, we cannot wag back, but we can smile and a dog will recognize this. He is responding to our body language in the same way that we observe and act on his. A dog's tail will also go between his legs when he is unhappy or in disgrace.

Experienced gamblers observe the tails of horses before a race. When the tail is arched so that you can see daylight between the base of the tail and the horse's rump, the horse is feeling happy and will race well.[4] However, it is a negative sign if the tail is arched and swinging back and forth. This means that the horse is upset about something and is not likely to be enthusiastic about the race.

Small children quickly learn that when a cat's tail swishes, it is a sign of anger. Cat's tails are extremely revealing. They twitch when they are stalking prey, and go straight up in the air when saying hello to a friend.

Although animals do not talk to each other in the way that we humans do, they use an effective combination of body language, sound, and mental pictures, or mind-to-mind communication.

As well as paying attention to your pet's body language, you must remain aware of your own. You are not likely to have good results if you are leaning over your pet in a manner that could be interpreted as threatening, or if your hands are crossed in front of you. Crossed hands are a protective gesture that frequently blocks telepathic communication.

AVOID STRESS

Both you and your pet should be free of stress when attempting any form of psychic communication. In all of the scientific experiments relating to psychic ability and animals, it was found that the animals achieved their best results in an environment of low stress. This is not surprising, as people also perform best when they are relaxed and interested in what is going on. If an experiment is attempted repeatedly, everyone, including your pet, will become bored and the success rate will drop. The best results occur when you stop while everyone is still fresh and interested, and continue at a later date.

MIND-TO-MIND COMMUNICATION

A few days ago, we visited friends who have two collies. The dogs lay sleeping at our feet as we talked. Suddenly, one of the dogs raised her head and looked at the other dog. This dog, apparently sleeping, instantly opened its eyes. A silent message was exchanged, because both dogs got up and began playing on the lawn. We humans heard nothing, as no sounds were exchanged. However, the first dog was able to tell the other one that it was time to play. This was obviously done by telepathically transmitting the thought of play.

Years ago we had a cat named Killy. As Killy got older she spent more and more time sleeping in different hiding places that she had found. We could search the house and garden, calling for her, and she would not respond. However, if we as much as thought about feeding her, she would instantly appear. Killy was reading our minds.

Killy and Bruce, our Labrador, would play together whenever Killy was in the mood. Bruce would have loved to play every day, but Killy would not allow this. When she felt like a game, she would sit beside Bruce and stare at him with a fixed gaze. Bruce would immediately wake up in a state of excitement and the two would play for half an hour or so. Once Killy had had enough, she would lie down and close her eyes. The game was always over far too soon for Bruce, but he quickly learned that it was no use trying to encourage Killy to continue. Barking and prodding her with his nose did no good. She never hissed or scratched him, but would leave the room and go to one of her hiding places. Consequently, once Killy announced that the game was over, Bruce would lie down beside her and go to sleep. Killy telepathically told Bruce that it was time for a game, and she also told him when the game was over. I am sure that Bruce sent telepathic messages to Killy pleading for another game, also.

Like all dogs, Bruce enjoyed offering love and sympathy to anyone in the family who needed it. Other humans can provide sympathy and understanding, but sometimes, when things go wrong, it takes a pet to provide the unconditional love that we crave.

Observe your pet for a day or two and see how many instances of mind-to-mind communication occur between you and your pet. You will be amazed at how common they are.

COMMUNICATING WITH YOUR PET

Naturally, you must attract your pet's attention. Your pet can read your thoughts whenever he or she wants to, but most of your thoughts are of no interest to anyone else, pets included. You might be thinking about asking your boss for a pay rise, or whether or not to buy a certain item that is on sale. These thoughts are important to you, but are of no interest to your pet. Consequently, your pets will pay attention only if something you are thinking about relates to them and they happen to pick it up.

You can communicate with your pet verbally or by thinking about what you want. Most people find it easier to talk out loud to their pets, as this is what they are used to. Ask your pet to pay attention and to listen to what you have to say. You can tell if your pet is paying attention, even if he or she is not looking at you. You might want to pet or stroke them before speaking to ensure that you have their attention.

Talk in terms of what you want your pet to do, rather than what you want them to avoid. For instance, if your dog is continually digging holes in your garden, you should not say to him, "Don't do that." Instead, you should talk about what you do want. You might say something like, "I have worked hard to make that garden look as beautiful as possible. I want it to look nice for when visitors call, and because it gives me pleasure to look at it. I know the ground in the garden is soft and nice to dig, but I'd appreciate it if you made holes somewhere else. Would you please help me by doing that."

There is nothing difficult about this. All you are doing is speaking to your pet and telling him or her what you want. There is no need to speak down to your pet, or to use baby talk. Your pet will respond best if you phrase your request in normal, everyday language. Your pet is extremely intelligent. He or she will understand. If you have been brought up to think about "dumb animals," you may have to change the way you think about your pet.

In his book *Kinship with All Life*, J. Allen Boone talks about establishing a two-way "mental bridge" between you and your pet. This invisible bridge allows thoughts to go from human to pet, and vice versa. However, it is important that the bridge be kept horizontal. If the human end rises, it means the person is talking down to his or her pet, and that means the end of telepathic communication.[5]

Of course, your pet may not want to listen to your request, especially if you are suggesting that he or she stops doing something he or she enjoys doing. This is especially the case if your pet walks away while you are talking to him or her.

If your pet is reluctant to listen to a specific request, you need to say it again while making direct eye contact. Hold your pet's head and gaze into his or her eyes. Explain the seriousness of your request, and why you are making it. Repeat your request, and then ask your pet for a response. Your pet might need several seconds to think about what has been said. The response might appear fully formed in your mind, or it might be a friendly lick on your face or hand. Rest assured that once your pet has given a positive reply, he or she will adhere to it most of the time.

Unless you receive a positive answer, your pet may choose to ignore your request. Humans do exactly the same thing. We may be asked to do something that we do not agree with. Rather than arguing about it, we might simply choose to ignore the request. Your pet will do exactly the same, especially if you are curtailing something enjoyable. However, once you have received a positive response you can relax, as most of the time your pet will keep his or her word.

You may want to provide a reward when your pet accedes to your requests. This does not have to be food. We usually rewarded Bruce by taking him on an extra-long walk. He always knew it was a reward and seldom tried to make me take him on the longer walk unless it had been earned.

Remember to follow up with praise when your pet has done something right. It is easy to do this immediately afterwards, but we tend to forget to do it after a day or two. It is good reinforcement to continue thanking your pet for his new behavior for as long as possible.

Working animals become extremely good at reading the minds of their human friends. I remember talking to a champion horsewoman after her horse had died. She commented that her horse had constantly read her mind. She had to simply imagine the two of them clearing a difficult jump and landing safely on the other side, and her horse would do it every time. This is an everyday occurrence for riders who have a close bond with their horse.

Blind people make similar comments, as they also have a close, intuitive connection with their guide dogs. Sheila

Hocken, a formerly blind lady in England, had an operation that gave her back her sight. She wrote a wonderful autobiography that told about her dependency on her guide dog. The book, *Emma and I*, became a bestseller. Sheila eventually wrote a series of books about her life with Emma. Sadly, Emma developed cataracts and became blind herself. With the roles reversed, Sheila dedicated herself to Emma's needs, repaying her for all the years of love and service that her dog had given her.

In *Emma and I*, Sheila told how she needed to make a telephone call shortly after moving to an apartment on her own. Emma guided her across the road to a public call box. When they got there, Sheila discovered that the phone had been vandalized and the receiver had been ripped off. Sheila told Emma this, and asked, "What are we going to do?"

Neither of them was familiar with the area, and Sheila asked Emma to take her along the road in the hope that they could find someone who could tell them where there was another phone box. Instead, Emma took her back across the main road and down a side road that felt rough and unformed. Later, Sheila discovered that building work was being done in the area. She tried to get Emma to stop and return home, but Emma continued down another road, and then sat down. Sheila felt with her hand and found that Emma had taken her to another phone box.[6]

Emma used her initiative in locating another phone box and taking Sheila to it. We cannot say that she located the second phone box by instinct. She obviously thought the matter through before taking her mistress on a walk that had a successful conclusion. Guide dogs are doing such things all around the world every day of the week.

In his book *Dog Psychology*, Tim Austin explains that many things can block the effective communication between owners and their dogs and vice versa. Moods, tempers, and poor timing are examples. He also insists that effective communication is a two-way process in which both dog and human are actively involved.[7]

LISTEN TO WHAT YOUR PET HAS TO SAY

"You never listen" is a common complaint that people make about others. You must ensure that your pet has no reason to think that you do not listen to what he or she has to say.

The most important part of hearing what your pet has to say is to simply remain receptive. Whenever you are stroking or cuddling your pet, think about the love you share and remain alert to any thoughts that pop into your mind. These may come as clear pictures, or simply as ideas. The response might even be a feeling in your heart, rather than a picture in your mind. Frequently you may not realize that the response has come from your pet, while at other times the thought could not have come from any other source. Remain impartial and accepting as the thoughts come in. If you react or become emotional, your pet will stop communicating.

A friend of ours is a well-known cat breeder. The intuitive bond she has with her pets is remarkable, yet she never receives thoughts or pictures. However, she is incredibly attuned to her cat's feelings, and responds to them the instant she receives them. A former neighbor of ours receives pictures in his mind, but only seldom receives thoughts or feelings. Everyone is different. It makes no difference what form the communication takes, just as long as you and your pet are able to understand and communicate with each other.

Many years ago we had two cats, Inka and Mika. Their feeding bowls were placed side by side in the kitchen, and they looked comical as they raced each other to see who would finish first.

One night, after placing their dishes down, I went through to the living room to watch the news. Ten minutes later, Inka, a Burmese, jumped on my lap and gazed at me. Suddenly, I received the thought that she was hungry. This seemed unlikely, as I had placed her food down only minutes before. I returned to the kitchen, closely followed by Inka, who meowed and rubbed against my legs. Both bowls were empty and Mika was nowhere to be seen. Rather reluctantly, I placed more food in Inka's bowl and she devoured it as if she had never seen food before.

The following evening, I fed them as usual. I then went through to the living room, as if I was going to watch television. Instead, I stood where I could secretly watch the two cats. Every time Inka tried to eat from her bowl, Mika would push her away. There was no need for her to hiss or snarl. Inka was the more passive of the two cats and meekly sat back and watched Mika eat her own meal, followed by Inka's.

Mika was smart enough not to do this when we were in the kitchen, but when no humans were around she greedily ate both bowls of food. If Inka had not put the thought of hunger into my mind, it might have been ages before we discovered what was going on.

Of course, there will be occasions when the message is not received clearly, or perhaps does not come through at all. Be patient. Your pet does not operate in the same way that you do. Simply enjoy being with your pet. Surround it with your feelings of love, and remain receptive to whatever comes. You might find it helpful to close your eyes while stroking your pet. Eliminating one of the senses tends to heighten the others, and I know many people who first achieved successful communication by doing this.

Be aware that thoughts are fleeting things that come and go in an instant. Do not evaluate anything that comes until afterward. If you stop to analyze anything, you run the risk of missing much of what your pet has to say.

Recognize that your pet is an intelligent being. Many people talk about "dumb animals" in a derogatory way, purely because they cannot communicate with words in the way that we do. Some people even refer to their animals as being dumb and unintelligent. It is unlikely that these people will ever receive a telepathic message from their pets. However, even these people can experience good results if they change their attitude. Our pets are much more intelligent than we realize, and will act dumb if that is what we expect from them. If you treat them as intelligent beings, you will receive intelligent answers.

You might want to ask your pet questions. I frequently say, "Is there something you want to tell me?" to our pets. Sometimes I'll receive no response at all. At other times I might receive a brusque "no." Every now and again, I will ask the question at exactly the right time and receive a detailed answer.

Our Siamese cat, Ting, enjoyed answering questions. I usually started by asking him how he was, and Ting would reply. Usually, I received a positive answer to this question, but sometimes he replied with a complaint. He might say that he did not like a certain brand of cat food, or that his basket was in a draft. I enjoyed his complaints, as it meant we could make whatever changes were necessary for his contentment and happiness. Ting was a typical, highly vocal Siamese cat, and his replies to my questions would come as a mixture of sounds, body language, and pictures. If I asked him what he thought of the cat next door, I usually received a snarl and a high-pitched yowl as a reply. I did not need any picture to understand the answer. Likewise, if he was tired and I asked him how he was, he would yawn and lie down, refusing to answer any further questions.

I seldom received thoughts from Ting without asking questions back. I think he enjoyed our lengthy conversations, which would have appeared strange to anyone who did not know what was going on.

Once you are experiencing a degree of success with your own pets, you should experiment with other people's pets. Some people find it easier to communicate with their friends' pets than their own. Seek out every opportunity you can to practice. Experiment with a variety of types of animals. Like everything else, the more frequently you experiment, the faster you will progress.

It is fun to practice with other people's pets and you can learn a great deal in the process. I go for a walk most evenings and enjoy a brief telepathic conversation with a tabby cat that lives a few hundred yards up the road. I have no idea who he belongs to, but we both enjoy the brief conversations we have. I miss him on the few occasions when he is not waiting for me.

Linda Thorssen, a friend of mine, is a professional animal communicator. She has a number of tips for people who want to communicate better with their pets.

1. Your attitude is extremely important. You must love and respect animals. You must consider them your equals. They are not inferior to you in any way. Any thoughts of that sort totally destroy the potential for communication.

2. If your pet is in the room with you, start out with a game, or a hug. A fun activity of this sort is beneficial on its own, but also makes communication easier. If your pet is not present, picture him or her in your mind, and say your pet's name telepathically. This will attract your pet's attention.

3. In the middle of the game, or the hug, think of something specific that relates to you and your pet. Usually, a thought about how much you love your pet is sufficient. Although the game, or hug, is still progressing, you will be able to tell by the look on your pet's face that he or she is listening telepathically, and is picking up your thought.

4. Continue with what you are doing, and wait for an answer to come. Listen. Trust what you receive. Your pet may not give you the answer that you want to hear. Once you have received an answer to your thought, you can continue with the conversation. Gradually, slow down the game until you are sitting or lying down together. If you began the exercise with a hug, keep on hugging until the conversation is over.

Linda also never hesitates to ask her angel guardians for help whenever she is having problems in communicating with an animal. "Obviously, I don't need to do this with my own pets," she explained. "But I enjoy talking with animals everywhere I go, and sometimes I need additional help."

Sadly, Linda also needs angelic help when dealing with animals that have been badly abused. "When people bring them to me, these animals are often trembling, whimpering, or appear badly cowed. Just recently, a woman brought a cat to me. Some teenage louts had been tormenting and torturing her. Eventually, they tossed her into a river to drown. The woman's young son had rescued her, and been badly scratched for his pains. Despite advertising in the local papers, they had not been able to find the cat's owners. The cat was getting better physically, but wouldn't let anyone touch her. The woman brought her to me, because she thought I might be able to help. The cat hissed at me when they arrived and sat on the floor as far away from me as she could. Her breathing sounded as if she had just finished a marathon.

"I started by sitting down in the room with her for several minutes, thinking pleasant thoughts about how much I loved cats. I then stretched out a hand, but she immediately backed away and hissed. Her eyes had a strange, wild look to them. I spoke soothing words and went back to my chair. Of course, I didn't really expect her to come to my hand. Sometimes it takes days before an abused animal will let a human touch them. However, it was worth a try.

"For several more minutes I sent reassuring messages to her. She was out of my field of vision, so I was not sure how she was responding to them. When the time felt right, I turned around to be greeted by another hiss, and a fierce meow."

Linda grinned. "I knew it was time to call in the artillery. I leaned back in my chair, closed my eyes, and called on my guardian angel for help. I don't actually see my guardian angel. I just know when he's there. It's a sense of 'knowing'. I can't explain it more than that.[8]

"When he arrived I asked him for help. I instantly felt as if the entire room had been filled with a clear, perfect white light. I kept my eyes closed for perhaps a minute.

When I opened them and turned around, the cat was sitting on the floor halfway between the corner and my chair.

"I smiled at her, noticing that her breathing had returned to normal. Her eyes no longer looked strange, and she looked into my eyes for the first time since we had met. I telepathically sent a message of love to her, and waited, and waited.

"Something was holding her back. I started to silently tell her that not all humans were bad, in fact most were good. She had been treated abominably, and I was sorry about that. If it was possible to find out who had done it, they would be punished. I told her that I was an animal communicator and my mission in life was to help animals. I would never consciously hurt any living thing.

"The cat kept staring at me. She was obviously receiving my thoughts, and paying close attention to them. Bad things have happened to me in the past, I told her. I'd survived a long-term abusive relationship and had felt just the way she did. It was hard to let it go, but eventually I had, as it was preventing me from carrying on with my life.

"She appeared absorbed in what I was saying. What you need, I told her, is lots of love. I am ready to talk any time you want. I am available to nurse and stroke and pet you whenever you wish. The people who brought you to me care about you, too. They have looked after you for more than a week, and you haven't even let them touch you. They want to love and care for you. You have a loving home to go to where you will be well treated and cared for. Would you like a home like that?

"I stopped then, and waited. It took a couple of minutes before a reply came to me. 'I can't trust people any more.' I don't blame you, I said. You were badly hurt and tormented. Please believe me when I say that these hooligans are the exception. You were unlucky to come across them, and I'd be surprised if it happened again.

"She looked away from me and then turned back with a different expression in her eyes. 'You will not harm me.' I don't think it was a question. It was more of a statement, and there was an element of surprise in it.

"I won't ever harm you, I said. And neither will Mary and Jason. If it hadn't been for Jason, you would probably be dead. And the two of them, and the rest of the family, have looked after you since. Would they have done that if they intended to hurt you?

"At that moment she stood up, stretched, and then came and sniffed my legs. When I felt her face rubbing against my clothes, I knew that everything would be all right."

It took several sessions for this cat to completely recover. She is still terrified of teenage boys, but is relaxed around other people, and is proving a wonderful pet to the family who took her in. Linda taught them how to communicate with her and the relationship is getting better all the time.

Linda has a few more hints for effective communication:

5. Ask your guardian angel for help at any time when you are dealing with animals. I am sure the animals are aware of your angel, and this makes communication that much easier to establish.

6. If the animal you are dealing with has been injured or abused, surround him or her with a healing light. I usually use a clear white light, but several people I know surround animals with a rainbow of light.

7. Ask your pet what he or she would like you to do to make his or her life better. Listen, and act upon the answers.

8. Send telepathic messages to your pet during the day, no matter where you are or what you are doing. Distance has no bearing on telepathy, and your pet will receive the message even if you are half a world away.

9. Be aware that communication can take place in a variety of forms. It may be thoughts, feelings, emotions, or a sudden sense of knowing. Be receptive, no matter what form the communication takes.

10. Practice, practice, practice. Like anything else, it takes time to become good at picking up the thoughts of your pets, and other animals. Practice whenever you can, and practice with as many different animals as you can. I tell my students to spend a day at the zoo. I don't approve of circuses or zoos, but they exist, and we can help those poor animals by being prepared to listen to their stories.

11. Enjoy yourself. Communicating with animals is the most worthwhile thing I have ever done. It is constantly rewarding, and I am forever learning. Many of my students are anxious and even fearful when they start. Once they relax and have fun with it, their progress is a joy to behold.

Many people wonder if they are actually receiving thoughts from their pets, as the whole process is simpler and more natural than they expected.

"For a long time I thought I was simply bringing up my own thoughts and feelings," Rhonda Miles, a student of Linda Thorssen, told me. "It seemed too easy. I couldn't believe that I'd spent almost forty years on this earth and never been aware of my pets' thoughts before. Yet, once I opened up my heart and allowed it to happen, the thoughts just flowed in. I noticed an immediate difference in my relationship with Oshi [her Abyssinian cat]. He began spending much more time with me, and he talked constantly. He had always been extremely vocal, but now he communicates with me telepathically as well."

If you take your time, and simply allow it to happen, you will be delighted with the results.

From ghoulies and ghosties and long-leggety beasties
And things that go bump in the night,
Good Lord, deliver us!
—SCOTTISH PRAYER

7

Ghost Animals

The close bonds that people have with their pets can even transcend the grave. Many people have told me of encounters they have had with their pets months, and even years, after they died.

A typical example was the experience of Rachel, a lady who was my secretary many years ago. Rachel lived on her own and was devoted to Mischka, her Burmese cat. When Mischka died at the age of eighteen, Rachel was heartbroken until Mischka visited her one night. Mischka had always slept on Rachel's bed, and Rachel enjoyed waking up in the middle of the night and feeling Mischka snuggled up against her.

Two weeks after her death, Mischka returned. Rachel woke up during the night and felt the pressure of Mischka's body against her. Surprised, she said, "Mischka, is that you?" Mischka instantly replied with a "brrrrt" sound, which had been her favorite greeting to Rachel throughout her life.

Rachel lay quietly, wide awake now, absorbing what she felt and heard. After several minutes, she reached out to pat Mischka, but there was nothing there. At first Rachel thought it was simply an incredibly vivid dream, but it occurred again the following night, and every night after that. Rachel began looking forward to her midnight chats with Mischka. After about three months, Mischka told her to get another cat. As soon as Rachel brought a small kitten home, Mischka stopped visiting.

Winslow Scanlen owned a small farm in Australia during the depression years. His dog Rover guarded the house and protected their small herd of goats from predatory dingoes (Australian wild dogs). One of Rover's jobs was to herd the goats into a special enclosure each night. In wet weather, the goats usually returned by themselves, but in fine weather they preferred to play. If the children of the house could not get the goats into the enclosure, Rover would do it.

Sadly, Rover was mysteriously poisoned. The children were heartbroken and insisted that Rover be buried close to the house. Without a dog to help, the task of rounding up the goats became especially difficult.

One fine evening, later than usual because the children had gone to bed, Winslow had to get the goats into their enclosure himself. The goats had had an enjoyable day and had no intention of letting him lock them up for the night. Winslow noticed Rover's grave and an idea occurred to him. If he whistled for Rover in the way he used to, the goats might think he was coming for them and stop playing around.

To his amazement, as soon as he whistled a ghostly form of Rover appeared and rounded up the goats, while Winslow gazed, speechless and mystified. The ghost dog waited until Winslow locked the enclosure, and then glided back to his grave.[1]

A well-known story that involves the spirit of a person, rather than a ghost, comes from India. When Sir Robert Grant, the governor of Bombay, died in 1838, people believed that his spirit had entered one of the many household cats. Unfortunately, no one knew which cat it was. Consequently, after sunset the sentries saluted any cat that came in the front door.[2]

The word "ghost" comes from the Saxon word *gaste*, which means "spirit." It is the soul of a dead person or animal that temporarily becomes visible to people who are currently alive. Some places are haunted, which means that ghostly apparitions frequent the site. Frequently, strange sounds are also heard. Examples include footsteps, rustling, sighs, knockings, and creakings. One of the most famous haunted houses was the infamous Borley Rectory in England that was burned to the ground in 1939. For many decades before then a large variety of ghostly apparitions were seen there, including a phantom coach and horses.

In their book *Psychic Phenomena*, Dorothy and Robert Bradley tell how their Chihuahua barked after he died to let the family know where he was. It was just before Christmas and the family was busy decorating the Christmas tree. No one noticed that the little dog had gone outside. When they discovered this, the family began searching for him, with no success. Dorothy continued working on the tree. The family was unsuccessful at finding the dog, but Dorothy was not worried, as she had heard him give a "series of shrill barks" seconds before the family returned. Dr. Bradley immediately thought that he was dead, and was giving a series of astral barks because that was his usual hostile reaction to anything unfamiliar. He went outside with a flashlight and found the dog frozen to death. Dr. Bradley had been inches away from the dead dog twenty minutes earlier, but had not seen him in the dark. Yet, fifteen minutes after that, the dead Chihuahua barked to alert the family to where he was.[3]

Mischka, Rover, and the Chihuahua were all loved family pets. However, there are also instances of ghostly animals that exist solely to protect a human they have had no previous association with.

One famous example of this is Gerigio, a phantom dog who loyally protected Don Bosco, a priest in Turin, Italy, in the second half of the nineteenth century. Don Bosco had dedicated his life to creating good citizens out of the wild, uncontrollable urchins of Turin. His work created many enemies, some of whom were prepared to kill him to prevent him from carrying out his good deeds.

Fortunately, Don Bosco had Gerigio, a huge, wolflike dog who appeared whenever necessary and attacked anyone who tried to harm the priest. On one occasion he even turned on the priest to prevent Don Bosco from leaving his hostel. Shortly afterward, a friend came in to warn Don Bosco of a threat on his life.

Many people tried to explain the mystery of this phantom dog. One of the more likely explanations is that Gerigio was Don Bosco's angel guardian who took on the appearance of a dog whenever necessary, as this was the form most likely to be of help.[4]

Another example of a companion ghost is recorded in *Cat Manners and Mysteries* by Nina Epton. An English lady was brokenhearted when her five-year-old Siamese cat was poisoned and died. A week after her pet died, the lady was first to arrive at the school where she worked. She walked down a long room that had large plate glass doors at the end. She could see her reflection in these doors. Walking beside her, tail held high, was her beloved Siamese cat. She could see nothing when she looked down, but could see her pet clearly in the plate glass doors. Her cat disappeared as she reached the doors. This ghostly companion gave her a sense of peace and comfort, along with a certain knowledge that she would see her pet again in the next life.[5]

Animals are also extremely good at sensing ghostly presences. When I was about twelve or thirteen, we visited a friend of my father's who managed a hostel for delinquent teenagers. The hostel was empty at the time, and we enjoyed having the huge building to play in. We children played hide-and-seek with our dog, Bruce. It was one of his favorite games and the new setting made it even more fun than usual. Late in the afternoon, I was hiding in a wardrobe with my brother and sisters, in a small bedroom on the second floor. It was a room we had not been in before. We heard Bruce running along the wooden floor of the hallway and into the room. He then gave a strange, blood-curdling howl. We peered out through a crack in the doors. Bruce was facing away from us, staring at the far corner, with his hair standing on end. He gave several low growls and slowly backed out of the room, the game completely forgotten. As soon as he was in the hallway, he raced back to our parents and sat as close to my father as he could, his tail between his legs.

We were puzzled by this. We clambered out of the wardrobe and examined the corner of the room that had so disturbed Bruce. We could see and sense nothing. We tried to entice Bruce into another game, but he was not interested. All he wanted to do was return to the car and go home.

My parents were busy having afternoon tea with their friend, but this strange behavior could not pass by unnoticed. The four of us excitedly told what we had seen. The hostel manager was extremely interested, as his cleaning lady had reported feeling strange whenever she was in that part of the building. Apparently, the former matron of the hostel had died in that room some years earlier, and Bruce was able to sense her astral presence. He promised to have the room exorcised, and wanted us to bring Bruce back after it hard been done to see if the procedure had worked. Unfortunately, my father's friend died soon afterward and we never returned.

Many children have "invisible friends." Parents usually put this down to imagination, and sometimes that is the case. However, not long ago, my wife and I were told about a three-year-old boy who had an imaginary friend he called Aunty Fay. There was no Aunt Fay in the family, and the boy's parents assumed she was simply an imaginary friend. One day, they noticed the strange behavior of their cat. Whenever Aunty Fay came to visit, their cat became agitated and wanted to be let out. He would not return until after Aunty Fay had left. Obviously, the boy and the cat were able to see things that the parents could not.

An interesting case in which the cat is the ghost was recorded in the *Proceedings* of the Society for Psychical Research. A Mrs. Gordon Jones had reluctantly agreed to have a cat in the house to kill the large number of mice that were living there. Mrs. Jones did not like cats and took no notice of the new addition to the household. One day, one of the servants told her that the cat was mad and asked if it could be put down. Mrs. Jones agreed and the kitchen boy drowned the cat in a boiler.

That evening, Mrs. Jones was reading in the dining room when something made her look at the door. The door slowly opened and in came the cat that had been killed that morning. It appeared to be completely drenched with water. Mrs. Jones wrote: "Only the expression of the gaze was not the same, for it regarded me with human eyes, so sad that I was pained; this look long remained impressed upon my memory as an obsession." Mrs. Jones rang for her parlor maid and asked her to take the cat away, but the maid could see nothing, and as Mrs. Jones watched "the cat began to become transparent and slowly disappeared."[6]

The famous British medium, Mrs. Gladys Osborne Leonard, was regularly visited by her cat, Mickey, after he died. One evening, a few weeks after his death, Mr. and Mrs. Leonard were reading in the living room, with their Pekinese dog, Ching, sleeping on the floor. Mrs. Leonard looked up and saw the astral body of Mickey sitting on a shelf beneath a table. She was about to draw her husband's attention to this when Ching began barking furiously. Her hair stood up, her eyes bulged, and "her cheeks puffed in and out with excitement." She rushed toward Mickey, who jumped out of the way, exactly as he had done when he was alive. He sat on a small side-table and looked down at the Pekinese who was jumping up and down trying to get to him.

Finally, Ching gave up and returned to her place on the hearth rug. Mrs. Leonard got up and went over to Mickey. She stroked him, noticing that apart from the fact that he was cleaner than ever before, he appeared to be exactly the same as he had been in life. Ching barked furiously the whole time she petted Mickey. Mr. Leonard was unable to see him. Mickey stayed for a few minutes after Mrs. Leonard had sat down again, and then vanished.

After this initial reappearance, Mickey visited Mrs. Leonard almost every night between eleven and eleven-thirty. When the Leonards were entertaining, Mickey would arrive, give a snort of disgust, and go away again.[7]

Mrs. Leonard was able to see the ghost of her cat. Cats are also extremely good at seeing ghosts of people. An interesting example that appears to demonstrate this was published in the London *Evening News* on October 5, 1923. H. G. Swindon, author of the article "What Did the Cat See?", returned home one evening, a week after his mother's death. His cat was distressed and was trying to escape from the room it had been shut up in. Mr. Swindon picked up the cat and placed her on his mother's favorite armchair. The cat had always loved this chair and leapt onto it whenever his mother got up. However, the cat no longer seemed to like the chair, and scratched her master on both hands in her haste to get off it. Mr. Swindon made three more attempts to place the cat on the chair, with no success. Mr. Swindon let the cat out of the room. She raced down the hallway and hid herself. From that evening onwards, the cat refused to sit on her formerly favorite chair. Nor would she stay in the room on her own. Whenever that happened, she scratched on the door until she was let out. Mr. Swindon finished his article with the words: "Could the cat have seen something that was invisible to human eyes?"

I mention this example as it appeared in print. However, there are countless other stories that could be told of cats who appear to be seeing ghosts.

Another one that I have witnessed myself occurred when acquaintances of ours were trying to sell their home. The young couple loved the house. They were selling it only because Marion, the wife, had come to believe that the house was haunted. Although she had never seen the ghost, she often felt a strange atmosphere in the house. At first she thought she was being overly sensitive, especially as Carl, her husband, could sense nothing. However, she felt partially vindicated when their neighbors told them that the previous owners had sold the house for the same reason. Apparently, an elderly man had died in the house several decades earlier. The story was that he could not move on until he felt that the right people were living in his former home.

Carl, the husband, remained skeptical until his sister and her family arrived to stay for a few days. They brought their cat with them. Horace was an elderly Persian cat who slept most of the time. However, he was unable to relax inside Carl and Marion's home. He roamed restlessly from room to room. In the spare bedroom his fur fluffed up and he hissed at something in the corner of the room. He growled in a deep voice that gradually increased in pitch. It took several minutes to calm him down. After that, he would go nowhere near this room.

Carl was still skeptical, but he mentioned the strange behavior of his sister's cat at work. One of his coworkers suggested that he bring his cat to visit, to see if she could sense the same vibrations. This cat was a young female cat of indeterminate breeding. She immediately made herself at home in the house and went straight to sleep in her master's lap. While apparently asleep, her master carried her from room to room. As soon as they entered the spare bedroom, she woke, jumped out of her master's arms, and began hissing and making strange sounds.

Intrigued now, Carl began inviting everyone he knew who owned a cat to visit. They all reacted in the same way in the spare bedroom. He began inviting friends with dogs to visit, as well. Only one dog, a Corgi, appeared to notice anything strange about this room.

Carl loved the house and was reluctant to move. He employed someone to exorcise the house, in an attempt to alleviate the problem. This worked for a short while. Immediately after the exorcism, cats appeared to notice nothing unusual about the haunted room. However, a few days later, the ghost returned.

Marion was pleased that Carl now believed in the ghost as strongly as she did, but still wanted to move. However, she now felt a responsibility for the invisible presence who was sharing their home. She told everyone that the house was haunted, and the buyer had to be a special person who would get on well with the ghost.

Naturally, this made the house hard to sell. One day, an elderly couple looked through it and made an offer. Marion asked them if they had a cat, which they did. She insisted that they bring the cat to the house. Their cat was small and timid. When they let him out in the hall, he went from room to room. He stopped at the entrance to the spare bedroom for some minutes, but seemed curious, rather than terrified. When Carl, Marion, and the cat's owners checked on him a few minutes later, he was curled up and asleep on the bed. This couple bought the house.

Ghostly animals abound in the folklore of most countries. When I lived in Cornwall I paid several visits to Dozmary Pool on Bodmin Moor. Back in the seventeenth century, there was an evil magistrate called Jan Tregeagle who sold his soul to the devil. He is now spending all of eternity emptying Dozmary Pool with a perforated shell. Every so often, the devil comes to see how he is getting on. The devil is always accompanied by a pack of headless hounds who chase the terrified former magistrate across the moor.

Cornwall is also the home of the Daisy Dog, a Pekinese who has terrified Cornish fishermen for centuries. I was told several versions of this story while living in Bodmin, Cornwall. There is an old legend that the Emperor of China sent a gift of two Pekinese dogs to Queen Elizabeth I as a token of mutual respect. Accompanying the valuable consignment was a royal princess, a mandarin to assist her, considerable gold, and a number of slaves. However, the trip was arduous and by the time they neared England all that was left were the princess, the gold, one slave, and the two Pekinese, plus a litter of puppies they had produced. The final section of the voyage was in a vessel crewed by Cornish fishermen. The weather became violent and everyone thought the ship would sink. The fishermen began thinking that the princess was an evil witch who would take them all to their deaths. Finally, they mutinied. They killed the captain, and then went to the princess' cabin. One of the crew reached out a hand to a gold-encrusted box, and quickly drew it back again with a shout of pain. One of the Pekinese inside the box had bitten him. The crew tossed the box and the princess overboard. Immediately, the wild seas calmed down and the ship was able to return to shore.

The dead princess and the box finally reached shore, too, and were cast up onto a deserted beach. No one would go near them, as the man who had been bitten had died a slow and agonizing death. Finally, a kind, simpleminded man saw the princess' body lying on the beach. He climbed down to see if he could help. He found the princess was dead, but something was moving inside a loose-fitting sleeve. It was the male Pekinese. The dog watched as the man opened the box and took out the bodies of the female Pekinese and the puppies. After consulting a priest, the man buried the princess and the dead dogs, and planted a cross of daisies on top. He then placed the surviving dog on top. The little dog licked his hand, lay down, and died.

Since that time, the ghost of the male Pekinese has been seen frequently, usually close to the gravesite. No one will approach him, because it is believed that if he bites you, death will quickly follow.[8]

There are many accounts of ghostly black dogs in Britain. They are often found at places related to death, such as graveyards and places where murders have been committed. They are also commonly found at crossroads, which were the traditional burial places of executed criminals and people who had committed suicide. This is because it was believed that the ghosts of these people would be less likely to find their way home if buried at a crossroads.

I originally thought these dogs were all called *shuck* (as shuck comes from the Anglo-Saxon word *scucca*, meaning "demon"). However, they are known by different names, depending on what part of the country they are found in. For instance, in Lancashire they are known as Trash; in Norfolk, Shuck; and in Yorkshire, Barghest.

Usually, these dogs mean no harm, and have been known to escort solitary women on their way home. However, there are some accounts that they can be harbingers of death. It is possible that these ghostly black dogs are the origin of the old saying "He has a black dog on his back," indicating someone who is depressed.

In 1927, on the Isle of Man, a black dog with long, shaggy hair and eyes "like coals of fire" met a man on his way home and refused to let him pass. The man's father died shortly afterward.[9]

These mysterious black dogs appear at night, usually in quiet country areas, stay for a short period of time, and then disappear. Many people have become aware of their presence after feeling the dog's hot breath on their necks. Still others have heard these dogs howl. Harry Mackall saw one of these dogs while living in Staffordshire in 1968.

"I was walking home at dusk and saw a black shape a hundred yards ahead of me," he told me. "I couldn't tell what it was at first. As we approached each other I saw that it was Padfoot (the name for such dogs in that part of the country). It was large, perhaps four feet high, and it had a shaggy coat. What I noticed most was his eyes. I couldn't tell you what color they were, but they seemed to glow, red one moment and green the next. I moved to the left-hand side of the lane to let it pass. I wasn't scared, as I didn't realize who it was until later. He seemed to nod at me as he passed. In that instant, I knew who it was. I turned to have another look, and he had completely disappeared. One second I could have touched him, and the next he'd completely disappeared."

My friend Stefan Dardik told me an interesting account of a ghostly horse. Many years ago, when he was a college student, Stefan enjoyed spending time in the desert area surrounding Santa Fe, New Mexico. One of his favorite places was a private ranch, often referred to as San Cristobal Ranch.

This site had been inhabited by the Tano Indians and abandoned during the Great Indian Revolt of 1692. At the time when Stefan was a student, it was a popular spot for nude sunbathing and swimming beside a natural pool with a small waterfall. Sadly, this idyllic spot is now overgrown and unused, with large "Keep Out" signs posted around it.

Stefan learned that the area had supported a large Indian settlement at one time. He explored the entire area, and was "eventually able to recognize ceremonial circles, little mounds that had been houses and much more." He spent a great deal of time searching for objects that had been washed out of the dirt by rain and erosion. He found pottery, bone needles, points, scrapers, and bones.

"I used to poke around one side near the top of a particular section of an arroyo [erosion break] which was widely separated by a ravine where a small stream flowed below," he told me. "Anyway, on numerous occasions, an extremely bizarre thing happened. As I would scan and poke the side of the arroyo's slope, about twelve feet up from the bottom of the ravine, I would hear the galloping hooves of a horse. At least, the speed and timbre sounded like a horse. The galloping grew louder and louder behind me, but whenever I turned to look, all I could see was empty air and no living thing on the ground for a long distance before me. The sound would grow louder and louder until it had all my attention. It sounded as if it was coming right at me, and then passed through me, carrying on up to the top of the arroyo, growing more distant and losing volume as it went further away.

"Sometimes this would happen as many as three times while I was spending hours there. Sometimes, it occurred only once, and other times not at all. I can only tell you that you would have to experience it. It felt so strange to have the sound come directly at you, envelope you, and then pass you. The whole experience lasted about three minutes, from the time I first heard the distant hoof beats, to the time when they had passed through me and faded away again.

"It sounded nothing like an echo, and I did not seek to find a natural explanation. I spent a great deal of time in this area and it did not seem to have echo properties. I don't discount the possibility that the area might have some strange acoustic properties. There are petroglyphs [Indian stone drawings] in the area that depict horses with enemy warriors riding them. I also found a small piece of pottery in the area that depicted a running horse. I file this case under 'very strange'."[10]

There are many accounts of ghostly horses that nightly roam across Europe, usually, but not always, with a rider. People are used to the sounds of their spectral hooves, the shouts of their riders, and the baying of the hounds that often accompany them. They are frequently referred to as *Hakelnberg* or *Hackelnbarend*, after a German knight called Hakelnberg. On his deathbed, he is said to have told the officiating priest that he had no interest in heaven because his only love was hunting. The priest was angry at hearing this, and told him, "In that case, you can hunt till Doomsday."[11]

A popular legend in Devon, England, concerns the ghost of Lady Howard (1596–1671), who travels around the countryside in a black coach drawn by black horses. The coach is driven by a headless coachman and a black hound usually runs ahead. Lady Howard's task is to pick up the people who are destined to die.

The folklore of many countries includes stories of people being carried around on ghostly horses. For instance, the ghost of an early French king regularly chases ghostly hounds in the forest at Fontainebleau. The ghost of Herne the Hunter still rides in the royal forest of Windsor. Odin still travels the Swedish countryside in a carriage pulled by horses. In Edinburgh, Scotland, a headless horse carries the ghost of a warlock, Major Weir, who was burned at the stake in 1670.

There is a difference between ghosts and apparitions. Ghosts tend to replay the same scene over and over again, as if they were endlessly acting out a play. They also tend not to interact with their environment. Apparitions are aware of their surroundings, and appear to be more "real" than ghosts. Some can even cast shadows or be reflected in a mirror. They have a disconcerting habit of appearing and disappearing suddenly, leaving their witnesses unsure of what they witnessed.

There is no need to be frightened of apparitions and ghosts. They have no interest in harming you. In fact, half of all ghostly sightings are over in less than sixty seconds.[12] However, as you are likely to see them at unexpected moments, it is natural to feel anxious or even terrified. Take several deep breaths to slow down your heart rate, and then ask questions telepathically. You can do this with the ghosts of both people and animals. You will be surprised at what you can learn.

Although these figures frequently appear solid and substantial, this is not the case. You will find that your hand passes right through ghosts and apparitions. You might feel a sense of coolness, but that is all.

Scientists frequently dismiss ghosts and apparitions, saying they are simply hallucinations. This is undoubtedly true in some instances, but there are many documented cases in which several people all saw the same apparition at the same time. It is impossible to believe that they all suffered the identical hallucination. The hallucination theory also does not answer the many cases where the ghost of a person comes to say goodbye before the people visited are aware that he or she has died. This type of apparition is called a wraith. A wraith usually appears once or twice, and is then never seen again.

Although it can be disturbing at first, most people who have seen the ghost of a departed pet find the experience comforting and beneficial.

HOW TO CONTACT A DEPARTED PET

Not everyone wants to communicate with a pet after he or she has died, preferring to remember the pet as he or she was in life. However, for many, it is a valuable part of the grieving process. Fortunately, it is a relatively simple task to send your love to your pet, even beyond the grave.

1. Sit down somewhere where you will not be disturbed. You may prefer to do this exercise while lying in bed at night.

2. Take three deep breaths, holding them for several seconds before exhaling. Allow your body to relax from

the top of your head to the tips of your toes. There is no hurry for this. Take as long as is necessary.

3. Think about some of the happy times you enjoyed with your pet. Try to visualize the scenes as vividly as you can.

4. Tell your pet how much you loved him or her, and how your life has been enriched by the times you spent together.

5. Send loving thoughts to your pet. Wait patiently, and you will receive love coming to you from your pet.

6. Send any special messages you wish to your pet.

7. At this stage, you can return to your everyday life, happy that you have communicated with your pet. Alternatively, you might want your pet to visit you one final time, as an apparition or wraith. You do this by asking your pet to come back and say a final good-bye. Wait patiently until you receive a response. This could come in many different ways. You may hear, in your mind, a meow, bark, or even the word "yes." You may feel a sense of knowing. You might even experience a gentle touch. Once you have made the request and received a positive answer, return to the present and carry on with your everyday life. Do not argue if the response is negative. You must respect your pet's wishes.

8. Thank your pet for the communication and return to the present.

Vanessa, a lady I used to work with, saw a wraith of her cat, Bascom, shortly after he died. Rather than comforting her, it increased her sense of loss. Consequently, I suggested that she contact him deliberately, using this procedure. Nothing happened the first time she tried it, but on the second occasion she felt Bascom rubbing his head against her leg.

"You wouldn't believe the sense of peace I felt," she told me. "Bascom was hit by a car, and I never had the opportunity to tell him how much he meant to me. I didn't see him when he came back, but I knew he was there. I was able to tell him how much he meant to me and how much I missed him. I'm sure he understood as I felt a wave of peace come over me. I still feel sad that he's not here with me, but I'm so grateful to him for giving us those last moments together. I can now move ahead in my own life."

I know many people who have benefited from communicating with their deceased pets in this way. This is particularly the case when the pet has died suddenly or tragically.

Do not try to hang on to your pet with these communications. Your pet must be set free and allowed to progress, and you must also carry on with your own life. The purpose of this exercise is to allow you to express your love to your pet, and to say goodbye.

Little Bo-peep has lost her sheep,
And can't tell where to find them;
Leave them alone, and they'll come home,
And bring their tails behind them.
—GAMMER GURTON'S GARLAND, 1810

8

Pets Who Find Their Way Home

Everyone knows stories of family pets who have been lost or left behind somewhere, and eventually managed to find their way back home. Most stories involve cats and dogs, but sometimes a surprising story appears in the newspapers. One that I found particularly touching involves a Friesian cow called Daisy who was sold at an auction in Devon, England. She was so upset at being separated from her calf that she jumped a gate in her new owner's farm and walked six miles across the fields to find her baby. Fortunately, her new owner was touched at the cow's maternal devotion and bought the calf so that they could be together.[1]

Another amusing anecdote also made headlines in March 1983. An eight-month-old sheepdog named Spot forced his way ahead of the line waiting to board a London-bound bus in Cardiff, Wales. He sat down on the front seat and growled at an inspector who tried to entice him out of the bus with food. Finally, the bus headed off to London with Spot on board. When they arrived, Spot got off with the other passengers and disappeared into the crowd. Shortly before the bus was due to start on the return trip, Spot reappeared and sat down again on the same seat. A reception committee from the RSPCA was waiting for him when he returned from his three-hundred-mile outing.[2]

There are many other stories that have been reported in the newspapers. In 1997, a cat named Shadow, from Pine Bluff, Arkansas, traveled ninety miles in ten days to return home.[3] In 1995, Chippie the cat left her new home in Marseilles, France, and walked the entire length of the French Riviera to her previous home in Nice.[4]

A sadder story, but with a happy ending, appeared in the newspapers in 1991. It involved a cat named Sam. In 1986, Sam's family moved from Wisconsin to Arizona. The following year they returned to Beaver Dam, Wisconsin, leaving Sam behind. Four years later, Sam returned, after a journey of 1,400 miles.[5]

Four years may sound like a long time, but Chester the tortoise took thirty-five years to return to his home in Lyde, England, according to newspaper reports in 1995. Malcolm Edwards, now aged forty-four, identified his childhood pet by a paint mark that his father had painted on Chester's shell.[6]

There have been a number of books written about some of the more remarkable of these exploits. One of these became a bestseller in 1926, when Charles Alexander's book *Bobbie: A Great Collie of Oregon* was published. Bobbie became lost while on vacation in Indiana with his family. Six months later he arrived back at his home in Silverton, Oregon, having somehow covered a distance of three thousand miles. Charles Alexander's detective work showed that Bobbie had spent short periods of time in Iowa, Colorado, Wyoming, and Idaho while finding his way home.

Sheila Burnford's book *The Incredible Journey* became a bestseller in 1961.[7] This book recounted the fictitious adventures of a Siamese cat, a young Labrador, and an elderly bull terrier as they traveled 250 miles home across rugged terrain in northern Ontario. This book was later made into a popular film by Walt Disney.

In 1973, a truck driver named Geoff Hancock stopped for a cup of coffee near Darwin, in the far north of Australia. While he was away, Whisky, his fox terrier, managed to jump out. Poor Whisky got lost, but eventually returned home to Melbourne nine months later, a distance of almost 1,800 miles.[8]

One remarkable case involves a dog called Tony. The family gave the dog to friends in a town near Chicago before moving to a new home in Michigan, some two hundred miles away. Six weeks later, Tony turned up at the new home, having traveled around Lake Michigan in the process. A locality tag he was wearing provided evidence of the route he had taken.[9] How did Tony know where the family had moved? This is one of those unanswerable questions that make the study of animals who find their way over long distances so fascinating.

The case of Sugar was so amazing that Dr. J. B. Rhine investigated it. Sugar was a two-year-old part-Persian cat who had been born with a deformed hip. When her owners retired in 1952, they moved from Anderson, California, to Gage, Oklahoma. As they thought that the 1,500-mile car journey would be too much for Sugar, they gave her to a neighbor. Sugar stayed there for just two weeks before setting out on a quest to find her owners. It took her fourteen months, which meant that Sugar, with a deformed hip, averaged more that one hundred miles a month over rugged terrain.[10]

The obvious question is why would pets want to track down and return to the people who apparently abandonded them? Obviously, in these cases there must be an exceptionally strong bond between the animal and the special people in his or her life. Some people are upset when their pet, usually a cat, returns to a house they have left, rather than settling down with them in the new home. In these cases, the animal obviously has a stronger connection with the place than with the people it lives with. However, if the bond is between the pet and the people, the animal will do almost anything to return to them.

Very little scientific research has been done in the ability of animals to find their way home. In the early 1920s, F. H. Herrick, a zoologist, became curious about the subject when his cat escaped from a travel bag when they were five miles away from home. The cat arrived safely home the same evening. Intrigued, Mr. Herrick began taking his cat to different locations that were from one to three miles from his home. The cat never had any problems in returning home.[11]

Ten years later, Bastian Schmidt, a German naturalist, conducted similar experiments with three sheepdogs. His first subject was named Max. Max was taken to various locations in a closed van, and secretly observed to see how he would return home. Max always began by looking in various directions. He would finally locate the direction of his home and would gaze homeward for up to half an hour. Then he would unerringly head home, avoiding houses, villages, woods, and cars in the process.[12] Herr Schmidt later conducted similar experiments in Munich with a dog called Nora. She also spent almost half an hour looking in various directions, but principally in the direction of her home, before heading in the right direction.

Dr. Rhine and his team at the Parapsychology Laboratory at Duke University also investigated the ability of animals to find their way home. Clementine, a young cat, was a good example. She walked from her former home in Dunkirk, New York, to her family's new home in Denver, Colorado, a distance of 1,600 miles. It took her four months, but she took time off to have a litter of kittens on the way.

One American test involved cats who were drugged before being taken well away from their homes. Once they woke up, they were tested to make sure that they had fully recovered, and then released. Amazingly, they always managed to find their way home.[13]

There have also been many reported instances of pets returning to their old home after the family has moved house. Cats do this more frequently than other animals. This has made some people think that the saying about cats being more attached to a specific house than the people who look after it is true. These people are unlikely to be cat lovers, and the suggestion is refuted by the fact that many more cats successfully track down their human owners in a new home than return to an old home.

There have been various suggestions put forward as to how animals are able to find their way home. Skeptics say that it is done using the animal's heightened sense of smell or because they remembered landmarks on the route. Herr Schmidt was convinced that his dogs did not use smell or visual cues. Definitive proof of this was provided by Troubles, an American scout dog in the Vietnam War.

Troubles and his handler, William Richardson, were airlifted into the jungle ten miles away from their base. Richardson was wounded and a helicopter transferred him to hospital. Somehow, Troubles was forgotten. Three weeks later, he was found back at base in An Khe. He was emaciated and exhausted, but would not let anyone near him until he had found William Richardson's belongings. Then he lay down and went to sleep.[14]

Another example, recorded by Dr. Milan Ryzl in his book *Parapsychology: A Scientific Approach*, is interesting as the missing dog had no sensory clues whatsoever to help him find his way home. The Burk's dog went missing on December 1, 1948. Shortly after that, the family moved to a new home 1,200 miles away. On November 27, 1949, their dog arrived at their new home. They recognized the dog because of a particular scar on one of his legs, and because of his likes and mannerisms.[15]

The only personal experience I have of dogs finding their own way home concerns our Labrador, Bruce. For the first few years of his life he roamed extensively around the city we live in. When he felt tired, he would befriend a human who would read the tag around his neck and phone us. My father would then pick him up and bring him home. Finally, after picking Bruce up every day for several weeks, my father got annoyed. He told the person at the other end of the phone to tell Bruce to "go home." We were all concerned about this as Bruce was several miles from home at the time. However, a few hours later, a tired and filthy Bruce barked excitedly outside our back door.

It took a few weeks, but once Bruce learned that he would not be picked up after his travels, he stopped roaming.

It is not known how pets are able to find their way home over long distances. However, in the wild such exploits are common. Wolves in the wild, for instance, cover huge areas and always find their way back to their dens. Homing pigeons, albatrosses, starlings, and swallows are all examples of birds that can travel enormous distances and safely return home. Bees are another example. The annual migration of many species is yet another. It seems that many animals possess an inbuilt homing device that enables them to find their way home.

This quality varies from animal to animal. Bastian Schmidt had great success with some dogs, but also tested others who were not able to find their way home.[16] This is not surprising. Humans, too, vary enormously in their directional capabilities.

People also vary enormously in their psychic perception. One person will use his or her intuition on a daily basis, while another may go through his or her entire life without ever noticing the still, quiet voice within. This might explain how some animals find their way home almost effortlessly, while others become hopelessly lost. Clairvoyancy may well explain why so many animals successfully find their way home. Obviously, much more research needs to be done in this area.

About the only thing we can say for certain is that we will continue to read stories in our daily papers of pets who have become lost, but do finally find their way home.

HOW TO HELP YOUR LOST
PET COME HOME

There are many accounts of pets that managed to find their way home. This is the positive side of the equation. Unfortunately, many other pets become hopelessly lost and never return. The loss of a pet is devastating, and I have met many people who are still suffering years after the disappearance of their pet.

Fortunately, if you enjoy regular telepathic communication with your pet, you will probably be able to locate him or her no matter where in the world your pet may be.

Sit down quietly in a place where you will not be disturbed, and send out a telepathic message to your pet. It is important that you remain as relaxed and unemotional as possible. This is not easy to achieve when you are concerned about a missing loved one, but it makes communication a great deal easier. If you feel unable to do it yourself, ask a trained animal communicator to locate your pet for you.

Send out messages of love and concern. Wait patiently to see what comes back. You may be fortunate and discover that your pet is just a few miles away. Ask your pet to describe the neighborhood, and then visit the area to see if you can find your pet. Put up flyers and ask people if they have seen your pet. Within a day or two, the two of you should be together again.

The reply you receive may be much more complicated. Your pet may have been stolen and taken hundreds, even thousands, of miles away. Ask your pet to describe the environment he or she is in. Ask as many questions as you can to try to pinpoint the area your pet is in.

As well as communicating telepathically with your pet, you should also send out regular telepathic messages while carrying on with your life. You might say something like: "I love you, and I want you back. Please make contact. We miss you terribly. Please come home." Visualize your pet surrounded by a protective white light and mentally see him or her hearing your messages.

Just recently, acquaintances of ours lost their Jack Russell terrier. They were extremely concerned, as over the previous several months many terriers had disappeared from their town. The police believed that they were being stolen to act as fodder in illegal dog fights. Apparently, as terriers were feisty dogs, people used them in practice fights to train their fighting dogs.

Fortunately, this was not the case with their dog. Margot lay on her bed and sent out messages of love to her dog. A faint reply came back, telling her that he had been taken by two small boys, and was less than a mile away. Margot and her husband searched the neighborhood and found their dog tied up in a garage. The children's parents had no idea of what they had done, and the boys' only response was that they wanted a dog.

It appears possible for pets to send back messages even after they have died. I have spoken with several people who received messages from their pets telling them that they had been killed, and that they were at peace.

"In my experience, between 70 and 80 percent of missing pets are dead," Rhonda Speer, a professional animal communicator, told me. "That may sound a high proportion, but you must remember that people come to me as a last resort. Normally, by the time they consult me, their pet has been missing for some time. I'm always reluctant to take on the job of finding lost pets, as far too often I discover that the pet is dead. If their pet has been stolen, I can sometimes describe the person who did it, and often tune in to where the pet is living. If the pet is living wild somewhere, I can tune in and describe the general area. All of that is extremely satisfying, which is why I love what I'm doing. However, I hate it when I have to report that their loved pet is dead."

Many times, an animal will choose to leave home. Clyde, our tabby cat, originally belonged to our next-door neighbor. When our previous cat died, Clyde moved in. We kept returning him, but by the time we had finished talking with our neighbor, Clyde would be back at our house.

The reason for this is that Clyde loved company. As I work at home, I could provide Clyde with companionship almost all the time. His owner was a busy accountant and frequently was away from home for sixteen or seventeen hours at a time.

Sometimes, though, a pet will choose to leave with no new home in mind. The pet might be annoyed at some change in the family arrangements. A newborn baby, for instance, may mean the pet no longer receives the same amount of attention as before. Perhaps a child in the household teases and torments the animal. A new pet may cause feelings of rejection and jealousy. There can be many reasons for a pet to leave.

In these cases, you will have to be patient. Tell your pet how much you love him or her. Listen to whatever it is your pet has to say. Find out what caused your pet to leave home. Correct the situation before inviting your pet back. Once you have done this, your pet is likely to arrive home within a day or two. Alternatively, your pet will be able to provide information that will lead you to wherever he or she is.

PET SAVIORS

I have met a number of people over the years who have an uncanny ability to attract stray and lost animals. One woman I know has helped dozens of lost cats to find their human families. She asked me why she was picked out for this task, as she knows no one else with the same ability.

We are all putting out energies all the time. People who love animals are sending that particular energy out into the universe. It is natural for a lost animal to pick up that energy, and find his or her way to that home.

Gladys has six cats that arrived on her doorstep at different times and stayed. They are all loved and well looked after. Yet Gladys considers them her failures, as she has managed to find the owners of every other cat who has arrived at her home over the years. As always, Gladys did everything she could to find their owners, but without success.

"They've all told me stories about their past," she told me. "It seems they were unwanted and unloved, and have no desire to go back to their previous homes. One even survived a drowning attempt. They get plenty of love here, and funnily enough, don't mind when a new addition arrives. These cats all know what it's like being lost, and, interestingly, appear to welcome any strays."

Gladys, and the others like her, are fulfilling an extremely useful function. She is gaining enormous satisfaction from helping lost animals, and loves nothing more than reuniting a lost pet with its owner.

There can never be enough pet saviors in the world.

In mythical times (before the Fall)
man lived at peace with animals,
and understood their speech.
—*Mircea Eliade*

9

Your Psychic Self

We are all psychic. Though you may not have called them "psychic," during your life you will have had many paranormal experiences. You are bound to have had the experience of knowing who was calling you before answering the phone. You have probably had moments when you knew exactly what someone was thinking. You may have walked into a room and immediately sensed tension and anger, even though the people already there were acting in an apparently calm manner. You will have experienced many hunches, or gut feelings. You may have had a premonition in the form of a dream. You may even have seen a ghost.

These are all psychic experiences, and they are just as natural as our other five senses. At the time, you may have rationalized these experiences or called them coincidences. Once you accept that there is nothing strange or unusual about sensing these things, you can open up the psychic side of your nature and develop it as far as you wish.

Much of the time we use our intuition without realizing it. We are constantly receiving information through all of our senses. The chances are that you and your pet communicate feelings of love in this way, even though you may not consciously be aware of it.

Your pet is naturally psychic. He or she does not turn it on or off. It is always there, and your pet makes good use of it every day. Once you allow your intuition to flow, the bond between the two of you will become closer and closer.

You are much, much more than just a physical being. You have a physical body, of course, but you also have an intellect and a soul. They all need your care and attention.

There is no point in looking after your physical body without also exercising your mind and spirit. Neither would it make much sense to focus on learning and gaining knowledge without also looking after your physical body and spirit.

Yet we all do this to a degree. We focus on certain parts of our makeup at the expense of other areas. Many people ignore, or even deny, the psychic, intuitive aspects of their being.

I have done this many times in the past. Whenever I ignore a gut feeling or a message that appears in my mind, I invariably regret it later. Some years ago I became involved in a property deal with a man who was extremely likeable and pleasant. He was charming, affable, and knowledgeable. However, there was something about him that my intuition picked up instantly. I experienced an immediate gut feeling that he was not what he appeared to be. I ignored this feeling, and lived to regret it. I am sure that I will continue to make mistakes of this sort in the future, but they are less common now, as I trust and act on my hunches and feelings much more than I used to.

Not long ago I met a man who makes his living playing the commodities market. He used to do this using cold, hard logic, but became much more successful when he started acting on his feelings. Whenever he feels tempted to buy or sell anything, he closes his eyes for a few moments and asks himself if he is making the right decision. When the answer is positive, he feels a sense of warmth and well-being throughout his entire body. If the answer is negative, he experiences a tightening sensation in his stomach.

"I still make mistakes," he told me. "But they are usually when I override my feelings and act entirely on logic."

PSYCHIC EXERCISES

The first step is to find a safe, secure place in which to experiment. For most people, this is a room at home. It can be anywhere, just as long as you feel safe and comfortable, and will not be interrupted while practicing these experiments. You may want to temporarily disconnect the telephone to avoid any possible interruptions. You need to be pleasantly warm, but not hot. You may wish to play some gentle mood music. I prefer silence, but many people enjoy having music in the background. Make sure that you have some pleasant objects in the room. These might be favorite ornaments, a painting, or perhaps freshly cut flowers in a vase. Dim the lighting. You can lie on the floor or sit in a comfortable chair. It makes no difference, just as long as you are comfortable and able to relax. Wear loose-fitting clothes. You may want to cover yourself with a blanket.

Many people like to make a tape of the relaxation exercise, as this allows them to focus on relaxing, instead of trying to remember what comes next. It makes no difference if you make the tape yourself, or have a friend record it for you. Some people feel that it is easier to relax when listening to a tape made by a person of the opposite sex, but I feel that it makes no difference, just as long as the voice is soothing and pleasant to listen to.

Some people like to start with a small ritual. They may light candles or burn essential oils. They might say a prayer, invoke their guardian angel, or sing a song. None of this is essential, but can be helpful if you feel it is appropriate.

Relaxation Exercise

1. Sit or lie down in your comfortable space.

2. Look around the room, allowing yourself time to pause and think pleasant thoughts about anything that catches your eye.

3. When you are ready, close your eyes and take a long, deep breath. Hold it for several seconds and exhale slowly.

4. Take another deep breath, and this time, as you exhale, allow yourself to relax all over. Enjoy the feeling of relaxation as it drifts through your body.

5. Take five deep breaths, holding each one for a few seconds before exhaling slowly. Focus on your breathing. Feel the breath coming into your body and down into your lungs. Hold it there for a few seconds, and then feel it leave again as you exhale. Some people feel that you achieve better results if you inhale through your nose and exhale through your mouth. In practice, I have noticed no difference. Do whatever feels right for you.

6. Forget about your breathing now. Focus on your toes, and allow them to relax. They may start to tingle before letting go. Once they feel totally relaxed, allow the relaxation to drift into both feet.

7. Slowly allow the relaxation to drift up your body. Pay special attention to your shoulders and neck, as a great deal of stress and tension gather here.

8. Allow the fine muscles around your eyes to relax, and then let the pleasant relaxation drift to the top of your head.

9. Mentally scan your body to make sure that every part is completely relaxed. Focus on any area that still seems tense and allow the relaxation to gradually eliminate the tension and stress. You are now totally relaxed.

10. Imagine yourself surrounded by a clear white light that enfolds and protects you. It fills you with confidence and happiness. Become aware that you can do anything that you wish. Think about a goal that you would like to achieve. Your goal might be to communicate telepathically with your pet. It might be something completely different. Think about this goal, and picture yourself, full of energy and enthusiasm, working on achieving it.

11. Enjoy the pleasant relaxation for as long as you wish. When you feel ready, count silently from one to five, and open your eyes.

You will find this relaxation exercise helpful in every aspect of your life. The exercise itself helps reduce stress and tension, and many people have told me that it has helped them clarify where they want to go in their lives.

Once you are able to relax quickly and easily, it is time to see yourself from a new perspective.

Psychic Awareness Exercise

1. Sit in a comfortable chair with both feet flat on the floor. Rest your hands on your thighs or in your lap. (This exercise can also be performed lying down, if you prefer.)

2. Close your eyes, and take a deep breath. Count to five in your mind, and then exhale slowly. Say to yourself, "Relax, relax, relax," as you exhale.

3. Take another ten slow, deep breaths, holding each breath for the count of five and exhaling slowly. Feel yourself gradually relaxing in every part of your body.

4. Become aware of yourself in this calm, relaxed state. Mentally move your consciousness out of your body and up to the ceiling in a corner of the room you are in. Look down on yourself. Visualize yourself as clearly as you can.

5. Move your consciousness into your head in the area between your eyebrows. Become aware of your body. Enjoy the regular rhythm of your breathing. Experience the sensation of the material of your clothes beneath your hands.

6. Take another three slow, deep breaths. Think of a pleasant experience from your past and experience it again, as clearly and as vividly as possible. Return to the present.

7. Feel yourself relaxed and contented and enjoying the present.

8. Think of an experience you would like to have in the future. Visualize it as clearly and as completely as you can. When you are ready, return to the present.

9. Count silently from one to five, open your eyes, and stretch.

This exercise is an extremely beneficial one in many ways. It enables you to become in tune with yourself, to go deep within and become aware that you are much more than simply a mind and body. Many people gain spiritual awareness when doing this exercise on a regular basis.

It will also help you to realize that you can achieve anything you set your mind on. Many people have no idea of what they really want out of life, and doing this exercise on a regular basis will enable you to gain a clear idea of what you want in the future.

This exercise also helps you develop your psychic awareness. While doing it, you will gain intuitive flashes about all sorts of things that are going on in your life.

After practicing the psychic awareness exercise for several days, you can then proceed to a more advanced exercise. This exercise is intended to allow you to communicate psychically with your pet. As a byproduct, it will bring you closer together, as well.

Becoming as One with Your Pet

1. Perform steps one to five from the previous exercise.

2. Think of your pet and your feelings for him or her.

3. Place your consciousness inside your pet.

4. Wait patiently and see what happens. You may receive a psychic message from your pet. Words may suddenly appear in your mind. You may feel a warm glow, or some other response. This is your pet sending you a message. You may receive a strong sense of what it is like to be a cat, dog, or whatever it is your pet happens to be. If your pet is in the same room as you, he or she might come over to you and lick your face, or give some other physical response.

5. Once you have received a response of any kind, allow your consciousness to return.

6. Thank the universe for enabling you and your pet to become even closer than before.

7. Count from one to five, open your eyes, and stretch.

With practice, you will be able to do this entire exercise in less than ten minutes. You will achieve better results if you do this exercise briefly on a regular basis, rather than spending half an hour on it once a week.

You can also use this exercise to determine the health of your pet. Mentally scan your pet's body while you are in stage four, and see what comes into your mind. If you find any areas of dis-ease, mentally surround the area with clear white light while sending thoughts of healing to your pet. Obviously, if you do find anything physically wrong with your pet while doing this exercise, you must have it checked out by a veterinarian.

In time, both you and your pet will welcome and enjoy the special closeness you derive from this exercise. You will find that your pet will send you a variety of messages. When you first start, these are likely to be feelings of contentment and love. In time you will receive much more specific messages. Your pet might be unhappy with something that a certain member of the household does. He or she might desire a more varied diet, a different bed, a new bone, or more frequent exercise. No matter what it is that your pet desires, he or she will be able to tell you about it through this exercise.

ANIMAL PSYCHICS

Animal psychics are people who can psychically tune into your pet for you. If you practice these exercises, you may ultimately become an animal psychic yourself. If so, you will be able to do valuable work helping people become more in tune with their pets. You will be able to diagnose illnesses, uncover and release psychological problems, eliminate behavioral problems, and perform a variety of other functions that affect people and their pets.

Linda Snow is a busy animal psychic who specializes in cats. She describes herself as a "cat person," so none of her friends were surprised when she turned her love of cats into a full-time career. Her only regret is that she is now too busy, and people have to book weeks ahead to see her.

"It was not a conscious career choice," she told me. "I worked in computers, and thought that was what I'd always do. I had several cats, and one evening when I came home from work, Sebastian, my Persian, was coughing. I thought he had hairballs. It was late, and there was nothing I could do except comfort him. I held him in my arms, and this amazing feeling came over me, as if Sebastian was telling me about his problem. It wasn't a hairball. He had something caught in his throat. In fact, it was a fish bone that had got stuck. I received a message to give him dry bread. I was worried sick that I'd make him worse, but it fixed the problem. By this stage, I was wondering if I'd really received a message, but when I picked Sebastian up again, I received a grateful thank you.

"I began holding my other cats in the same way, and asking them how they felt. To my amazement, they all responded. It was ages before I told anyone about it, but one of my friends was extremely encouraging. In fact, she virtually pushed me into this business, as I was so reluctant to let go of what I'd always done. She had a cat, a huge tom. I thought he'd scratch me, but he settled down in my arms. He told me about something that was missing in his diet. I couldn't have been more surprised. Anyway, my friend gave him what he was missing, and he improved out of sight. She told another friend, and before I knew where I was, I was seeing cats almost every night. I fought it all the way. I was happy in computers. But you know, my life really began when I started doing this full-time. I feel that finally I'm doing something worthwhile."

Fortunately, today there are many people working as animal psychics. Twenty years ago this would have been considered an unusual occupation. I remember a man in Brighton, England, who started giving psychic readings for animals in the early 1970s. He received a great deal of press publicity, because what he did was newsworthy at the time. Fortunately, pet psychics are no longer considered strange or unusual, and it would be hard to think of a more satisfying or valuable career.

Obviously, you need to have a great love for, and respect of, animals to even consider becoming an animal communicator. You also need to believe that you can successfully communicate telepathically with animals. You need to be prepared to practice for as long as is necessary to perfect your skills. You need to practice listening, really listening, to what the animals have to say. You need to be able to focus entirely on the animal you are working on until you have finished your evaluation. You need to be gentle, caring, and empathetic. If you are prepared to do this, you have the potential to improve the lives of countless people and animals.

The best way to become an animal psychic is to allow it to gradually develop. Listen carefully. Communicate with as many animals as you can, and see what information comes to you. Determine which animals you enjoy working with most. You may decide to specialize in one particular animal.

Bill Northern is a horse psychic in Virginia who works internationally. He is often called in when a racehorse is not performing as well as he or she should be. Bill discovered his talents while learning how to dowse in Vermont. His instructors had two horses and Bill had to answer twenty questions about each horse. He failed, but had become fascinated with the process, and went home to practice. One day, he walked into a stable and a horse told him that it had not been given an apple that day. The horse's owner denied this, but then realized that it was true. This simple start set Bill on a career that has taken him around the world.

Bill has a special empathy with horses, which is why he specializes in them, but he receives messages from other animals, as well. In fact, he hears from so many animals that he has to deliberately block them out, unless he is able to help them.[1]

You might want to use the services of a professional animal communicator. The best way to find one is by word-of-mouth recommendation. Find out as much as you can about the communicator before employing them. Ask for letters of recommendation, and call a few of their clients to see how happy they were with the communicator's services.

If you are unable to find an animal communicator by word-of-mouth, there is an excellent newsletter called *Species-Link: A Journal of Interspecies Communication*. This lists recommended animal communicators in the United States.[2]

And so, as I sleep, some dream beguiles me
and suddenly I know I am dreaming.
Then I think: This is a dream, a pure diversion
of my will; and now that I have unlimited power,
I am going to cause a tiger.
—*JORGE LUIS BORGES*

10

Communicating with Your Pet
In Dreams

People have always been fascinated with their own dreams. The Bible contains many accounts of dreams and dream interpretations. The ancient Egyptians appear to be the first people to study dream interpretations, and the Greeks took it to new heights, paying special attention to the symbolisms and prophetic nature of dreams.

At the end of the nineteenth century, psychologists began studying dreams. Dr. Sigmund Freud believed that dreams were largely wish fulfillment, and that most of the time we dreamed about sex, followed by birth and death. Dr. Carl Jung took a much broader view of the subject, and believed that we usually dream about situations that are the opposite of what we experience in everyday life.

Parapsychologists have been studying dreams for more than a hundred years. Dr. Louisa Rhine collected thousands of accounts of precognitive dreams in the course of her research. It appears that intuitive dreams are common and everyone experiences them. It is not known why people are apparently more psychic in their sleep than they are while they are awake. It is possible that we are receiving psychic impressions all the time, but tend to ignore them while we are awake because our conscious minds are engaged on other things.

In the early 1950s, two American researchers, William Dement and Nathaniel Kleitman, discovered that at different times in our sleep, our brain waves were almost as fast as they are when we are awake, and that our eyes moved rapidly from side to side. People remembered dreaming if they were woken up during one of these REM (rapid eye movement) stages. However, if they were woken at times when the REM was not occurring, they usually reported that they were not dreaming.

Since 1972, the researchers at the Maimonides Dream Laboratory in New York have been studying telepathic and precognitive dreams in a laboratory setting. Some of the results have been incredible. One night, Malcolm Bessant, one of their best subjects, dreamed about buying tickets to a boxing match at Madison Square Garden. The target picture that was being telepathically sent to him in his sleep was a picture of a boxing match.[1]

Over the last forty years, scientists have been studying and researching the timing of dreams and the specific brainwaves that are produced at the time the dream state occurs. Today, interest in dreams is greater than ever.

In fact, dreams have changed the course of the world's history. If Mohammed had ignored the advice of the angel Gabriel, who appeared to him in a dream, he would not have conquered Mecca and the spread of Islam may not have occurred. Genghis Khan had a dream in which he was told that he would rule over the Mongols. In more modern times, Bismarck decided to invade Austria as the result of a dream. Doris Kearns, an aide to President Lyndon B. Johnson, believes that his decision to withdraw from Vietnam was the result of a dream.[2]

There are many different types of dreams. These are examples of precognitive dreams, as they give the dreamer a glimpse into the future. Nightmares are dreams based on fear. Inspirational dreams can solve problems that puzzled us while we were awake. This is why we so often wake up in the morning with the answers to problems that were unsolvable when we went to bed. Telepathic and clairvoyant dreams give us psychic insights into the motivations and behaviors of others. In the same way that we communicate telepathically with people, we can communicate telepathically with our pets in our sleep. The problem, of course, is remembering the dream once we wake up.

Fortunately, dream diaries can help with this problem. While lying in bed waiting for sleep to come, tell yourself that you will remember your dreams in the morning.

When you wake up, you will recall something of the dreams you had. Write these down as quickly as you can. While you are doing this, you will probably remember more details of your dream, and sometimes the entire dream will come back to you. It takes practice to become good at this, but once you do, your dream diary will become an extremely valuable resource that will help you in many areas of your life.

You can also tell yourself before going to sleep that you will dream about your pet. You can be much more specific than this, too, if you wish. You might want to have a conversation with your pet in your dreams. You might decide that you want to dream about your pet and find out why he or she behaves in a certain way. Maybe your pet dislikes someone and you want to know why. Perhaps your pet has been behaving strangely and you want to find out what is responsible for this change in behavior. It makes no difference what the problem is. The answers can frequently be found as a result of dreams that are directed in this way. If the answer does not come to you when you wake up the next morning, keep on requesting the same dream every night until you do receive an answer.

It is likely that you figure in your pet's dreams also, as it is now known that animals dream about actual experiences in their lives. Researchers at the Massachusetts Institute of Technology (MIT) have found that animals have lengthy, complex dreams that relate to everyday experiences.

In an interesting experiment, Matthew Wilson, associate professor of brain and cognitive sciences at MIT, and graduate student Kenway Louie taught trained rats to run around a circular track to receive a food reward. The rats' brain activity was monitored while they were running, and while they were asleep. While the rats were running, the brains created a unique pattern of neurons in an area of the brain related to memory. The researchers then examined more than forty REM episodes while the rats were sleeping. Most dreams occur, in animals and humans, in the REM state. In about half of the REM episodes that were monitored, the rats duplicated the same brain activity that they had registered while running around the track. In fact, the similarities were so close that the researchers found that they could determine exactly whereabouts in the track the rat was in the dream, and if he or she was running or standing still.[3]

LUCID DREAMING

Lucid dreams are a special type of dream in which you are aware that you are dreaming, and can direct the dream in any direction you wish. It is a facility that anyone can develop with practice.

The term "lucid dream" was coined by Frederik Van Eeden, a Dutch physician, in 1913. He began studying his own dreams in 1896, and had his first lucid dream one year later. However, the first book to include information on what he called "guided dreams" was written by the Marquis d'Hervey de Saint-Denys, a French professor of Chinese literature, in 1867. He became interested in dreams at an early age and started a dream diary at the age of thirteen. He soon discovered that, as time went on, he remembered more and more details about his dreams. He also discovered that sometimes, while he was dreaming, he was aware that he was dreaming and could make the dream go in any direction he chose. The more he practised this, the more frequently it occurred, until he could dream lucidly whenever he wished.[4]

People who are interested in their dreams tend to dream lucidly on a regular basis. People who have no interest in their dreams tend not to remember them and usually do not experience lucid dreams. Consequently, a good first step to lucid dreaming is to pay attention to your dreams by keeping a dream diary.

Most people find it best to experiment in the weekend, when they do not have to get up at a specific time the following morning. Make sure that you do not overeat or drink to excess before experimenting with lucid dreaming.

I have included a number of methods to experience a lucid dream. This is because no one method seems to work for everyone. Try them all and see which method works best for you. Like anything else worthwhile, it takes time, patience, and hard work to succeed, but the rewards are well worth the effort.

Method One

A recurring dream provides a useful stepping-stone to a lucid dream. If you dream the same dream regularly, tell yourself before going to sleep that when you start to experience this dream again, you will move directly into a lucid dream.

Method Two

The recurring dream method is useful only for people who experience them. However, you can use a similar technique to enter into a lucid dream. Before falling asleep, tell yourself that when you experience a certain situation or see a specific object in your dream, you will immediately become aware of it and enter into a lucid dream. The situation or object can be anything at all. Go through your dream diaries and see what situations, objects, or symbols appear on a regular basis. It might be a physical object, such as a car or a hand. Alternatively, it could be a feeling or emotion.

Method Three

Another method that works well for some people is to tell yourself before drifting off to sleep that you will experience a lucid dream that night. You need to repeat this to yourself several times before dropping off to sleep.

Method Four

An alternative method is to find a few minutes, several times a day, in which you can relax. Close your eyes, take several deep breaths, and relax as much as you can. Tell yourself that you will experience a lucid dream in your sleep. Do this as frequently as possible until you start experiencing lucid dreams.

Method Five

A number of people have told me that they lucid dream more easily if they have a cup of herbal tea before going to bed. Chamomile tea seems to work well.

Method Six

This method involves staring at a fixed object for several minutes before falling asleep. Keep focused on the object while telling yourself that you will experience a lucid dream.

Method Seven

This method works well for people who have had little success with the other methods. It involves going to sleep at a time when you would normally be awake. You are more likely to lucid dream while taking an afternoon nap, for instance, than you are when sleeping soundly during the night. This is because you will not sleep as deeply in your nap, and are more likely to recognize a lucid dream when it occurs.

Method Eight

When you go to bed, set your alarm clock to wake you after four hours of sleep. As we experience more periods of REM sleep in the second half of each night, lucid dreams are much more likely to occur in the three or four hours before we get up in the morning. By deliberately waking yourself, and then going back to sleep again with the intention of experiencing a lucid dream, you are more likely to experience one.

Method Nine

A final method involves using a hypnotherapist to help you get started. In hypnosis you enter a trance state in which you can experience two levels of reality at the same time. A good hypnotherapist will let you experience this and then provide suggestions that will help you experience a lucid dream in your sleep. Of course, in a lucid dream you are experiencing three levels of reality at the same time: you are aware of your physical body lying in bed, you are aware of what is happening in your lucid dream, and you are aware that you are observing yourself in the dream.

Experiencing a Lucid Dream

Once you become aware that you are dreaming, you can experiment in any way you wish. You can continue with the dream you are having, and see where it takes you. You might decide to visit your workplace or have a conversation with a deceased relative. It may seem as if there is no limit to what you can do, but there are some constraints. You may find it impossible to change the landscape, for instance, even though you are able to control everything inside it. You will learn from experience what you can and cannot change.

I am assuming that you are learning how to lucid dream mainly to become closer to your pet. You will be able to summon your pets to you in the course of a lucid dream. You may find yourselves in an environment that is strange and unusual, but this does not matter. Once your pet has arrived, see yourself doing something with him or her. It might be a normal, everyday experience, such as taking your dog for a walk or riding your horse. Everything is enhanced in a lucid dream, and you will experience it all vividly, in glorious color and perfect detail.

As it is a dream, of course, you can talk freely with your pet and he or she will give you complete answers, sometimes in enormous detail. This conversation will seem perfectly normal to you, and you will be surprised at some of the answers you receive. You will be able to ask your pet about his or her hopes and dreams. You will be able to indulge in some of your pet's favorite activities, and perhaps lie down and relax with your pet for a while before drifting back to sleep again.

One of the best aspects of a lucid dream is that you will remember it all clearly when you wake up in the morning. It will seem as vivid as if it all happened while you were awake, rather than in the dream state.

There are no boundaries, either. You can just as easily spend time in a lucid dream with a pet from your childhood as you can with a current pet. You can spend time with anyone or anything you wish in a lucid dream.

Once you are able to lucid dream, you will find yourself wanting to do it all the time. In fact, many people become addicted to it because they prefer their wonderful dream world to reality. The problem with this is that important matters in the everyday world are left unattended while the person dreams his or her life away.

It is best to deliberately seek a lucid dream once or twice a week, and have a specific purpose in mind each time. You may experience involuntary lucid dreams every now and again as well, and there is nothing wrong with that. People who "overdose" on lucid dreams find that the wonderful colors, feelings, and experiences lose their intensity after a while. Fortunately, they return to their former brilliance after the person has had a rest from lucid dreaming for a while.

No one knows why this occurs, but it is possible that because we dream for specific reasons, we are not meant to seize our dreams and control them all of the time. Sooner or later, if we keep doing this, the source of the dreams will step in and take charge again. Consequently, make the most of lucid dreaming to help you become closer to the important animals and people in your life, but do not allow yourself to become dependent on them.

Lucid dreams are always enjoyable experiences. None of the unpleasant elements that frequently occur in normal dreams, such as being chased or falling, are present. Everything is more vibrant than in normal dreams and in real life. Lucid dreams can be highly emotional, but again, these emotions are always positive.

Other Animals

You may meet other animals in the course of your lucid dreaming. You may know some of these, but others will be unfamiliar. You might even see some strange, imaginary animals. Fortunately, in a lucid dream, they will be good-natured and nonthreatening.

You might even see a horse winning a race a day or two before it occurs in real life. Wilbur Wright, the novelist, had three experiences of this, but unfortunately did not bet on any of the horses. He told his friends about his dreams, and they made money each time. The first two dreams of this sort were not lucid dreams. Wilbur experienced himself at a racecourse with an unknown companion at his side. In each dream he had a conversation with this man to determine which horse had won the race. On the third occasion, Wilbur realized that he was dreaming and experienced a lucid dream. He turned to his anonymous companion and said, "Oh no! Not you again!" He then carried on with the usual conversation about who had won the race.[5]

Animals are considered positive symbols in dreams, and you will find that in your lucid dreams you can enjoy lengthy conversations with them.

A NEW WORLD

You may find some of the ideas in this book hard to accept at first. However, I am sure that you will notice an immediate change in your relationship with your pet once you start to practice the ideas outlined here. Your pet is psychic and will welcome the additional closeness that the two of you will enjoy in the future. No matter how good your relationship may be now, it will reach new heights as soon as you have a full psychic connection with your pet. This will be extremely useful in everyday life, and you will also be able to remain in close communication even when you are separated by thousands of miles.

There are other advantages, also. You will know immediately if your pet likes, or dislikes, a certain type of food. At one time we had a greedy Siamese cat who ate everything put in front of her. We were surprised, to say the least, when we discovered that she did not enjoy a certain brand of cat food. She always ate it, which is surprising, as no other cat we have had would have eaten something he or she did not enjoy. Naturally, once we learned that she did not like this particular food, we stopped buying it for her.

There are more important advantages, also. If your pet is unwell, for instance, he or she will be able to let you know about it much more quickly than before. In severe cases, this could even save your pet's life. Conversely, your pet could also save you. In this book I've included examples of people who were alerted to danger by their pets. When you develop a close, intuitive relationship with your pet, you will be more aware of any changes in your pet's behavior, and will be able to take advantage of it in cases of danger.

You will also find your relationships with all living things will improve. You will start communicating with animals everywhere you go. You will see everything in a different way, and realize the interconnectedness between all living things. Your faith and philosophy of life will grow exponentially as you experience this and discover that we are all aspects of the one Self.

Take your time with the various tests. Your pet will welcome them, but may be surprised at your sudden interest in the subject. Do not expect miracles right away. With the help of your pet, you will learn to appreciate animal perceptions and their amazing senses, including, of course, their incredible sixth sense. In the process, you will unlock and release your own intuition. Your pet is willing to open your eyes to a whole new world. All you need do is listen.

NOTES

Introduction

1. Erika Friedmann, Aaron H. Katcher, Sue A. Thomas, James J. Lynch, and Peter R. Messent, "Animal Companions and One-Year Survival of Patients After Discharge from a Coronary Care Unit," *Public Health Report* 95 (1980): 307–312.

2. Aaron Honori Katcher and Alan M. Beck, *New Perspectives on Our Lives with Companion Animals* (Philadelphia, Penn.: University of Pennsylvania Press, 1983), 532.

3. E. Ormerod, "Pet Programmes in Prisons," *Society for Companion Animal Studies Journal* 8 (4, 1996): 1–3.

4. Paulette Cooper and Paul Noble, *277 Secrets Your Dog Wants You to Know* (Berkeley, Calif.: Ten Speed Press, 1995), 95.

5. Bernard Asbell, *The Book of You* (New York, N.Y.: Ballentine Books, 1992), 238. (Originally published as *What They Know About You* by Random House, Inc., New York, 1991.)

6. Dr. Stanley Coren, *Why We Love the Dogs We Do* (New York, N.Y.: The Free Press, 1998), xi.

7. Dr. Bruce Fogle, "Unexpected Dog Ownership Findings from Eastern Europe," *Anthrozoos* 7: 270.

8. U.S. Census Bureau, www.census.gov/statab/www/freq/html.

9. Carl Wyndcliff, *Stories of Famous Authors* (London, UK: Congreve and Company Limited, 1922), 173.

10. Richard St. Barbe Baker, "Dog Sense," *Dogs That Serve*, compiled by L. G. Cashmore (London, UK: George Ronald, 1960), 31.

11. Dr. Rupert Sheldrake, *Dogs That Know When Their Owners Are Coming Home and Other Unexplained Powers of Animals* (London, UK: Hutchinson, 1999), 12–14 and 257–271.

Chapter One

1. Warren D. Thomas and Daniel Kaufman, *Elephant Midwives, Parrot Duets and Other Intriguing Facts from the Animal Kingdom* (London, UK: Robson Books, 1991), 86.

2. R. McNeill Alexander, *Animal Mechanics* (Oxford, UK: Blackwell Scientific Publications, 1983), 277–278.

3. Sarah Heath, *Why Does My Cat . . . ?* (London, UK: Souvenir Press Limited, 1993), 129.

4. Gary Brodsky, *The Mind of the Cat* (Stamford, Conn.: Longmeadow Press, 1990), 32.

5. Warren D. Thomas and Daniel Kaufman, *Elephant Midwives, Parrot Duets and Other Intriguing Facts from the Animal Kingdom*, 58.

6. Ibid., 58.

7. John Downer, *Supersense* (New York, N.Y.: Henry Holt and Company, Inc., 1988), 8.

8. Ibid., 25.

9. Warren D. Thomas and Daniel Kaufman, *Elephants' Midwives, Parrot Duets and Other Intriguing Facts from the Animal Kingdom*, 86–87.

10. James L. Gould and Carol Grant Gould, *The Animal Mind* (New York, N.Y.: Scientific American Library, 1994), 71–72.

11. Rolf Harris, *Tall Animal Tales* (London, UK: Headline Book Publishing, 2000), 213.

12. Martin Ebon, *Prophecy in Our Time* (New York, N.Y.: The New American Library, Inc., 1968), 174.

13. A. H. Crowther, "The Mysterious Warning," *Authentic Stories of Intelligence in Animals,* collected by Geoffrey Hodson (Auckland, NZ: The Council of Combined Animal Welfare Organizations of New Zealand, n.d.), 49.

14. John J. Kohut and Roland Sweet, *Strange Tails: All-Too-True News from the Animal Kingdom* (New York, N.Y.: Penguin Putnam, Inc., 1999), 34.

15. Diodorus of Sicily (12 volumes), translated by Charles L. Sherman (Cambridge, Mass.: Harvard University Press, 1952), Volume 7, 81–89.

16. Pliny the Elder, *Historia Naturalis* 2, 84.

17. D. de Dolomieu, *Memoire sur les tremblements de terre de la Calbre pendant l'annee 1783* (Rome, Italy, 1784), 131–133.

18. *Time Magazine* (January 24, 1977): 26.

19. Helmut Tributsch, *When the Snakes Awake: Animals and Earthquake Prediction* (Cambridge, Mass.: The MIT Press, 1982), 64–65 and 234–235.

20. Stuart Gordon, *The Paranormal: An Illustrated Encyclopedia* (London, UK: Headline Book Publishing Plc., 1992), 23.

21. Stan Gooch, *The Secret Life of Humans* (London, UK: J. M. Dent & Sons Limited, 1981), 106–107.

Chapter Two

1. M. Oldfield Howey, *The Cat in Magic, Mythology, and Religion* (New York, N.Y.: Crescent Books, 1989), 198. (Originally published by Rider and Company, London, as *The Cat in the Mysteries of Religion and Magic*.)

2. "Purrfectly Wonderful Way to Be Healthy," unattributed article in *The New Zealand Herald*, March 20, 2001.

3. Richard Webster, *Dowsing for Beginners* (St. Paul, Minn.: Llewellyn Publications, 1996), 107–108.

4. M. Oldfield Howey, *The Cat in Magic, Mythology, and Religion*, 202–203.

5. Yvonne Roberts, *Animal Heroes* (London, UK: Pelham Books/Stephen Greene Press, 1980), 59–60.

6. DeTraci Regula, *The Mysteries of Isis* (St. Paul, Minn.: Llewellyn Publications, 1995), 137.

7. Cornfield Parrish, *Persian Myths and Legends* (London, UK: The Cranston Company, 1922), 342.

8. Patricia Dale-Green, *The Cult of the Cat* (New York, N.Y.: Weathervane Books, n.d.), 118. (Originally published by Houghton Mifflin Company, 1963.)

9. Ibid., 143.

10. Howard Loxton, *99 Lives: Cats in History, Legend and Literature* (San Francisco, Calif.: Chronicle Books, 1998), 120.

11. J. J. M. de Groot, *The Religious System of China* (Originally published in 1892. Reprinted by Literature House Limited, Taipei, Taiwan, 1975), v and 825.

12. Zolar, *Zolar's Encyclopedia of Omens, Signs and Superstitions* (New York, N.Y.: Prentice Hall Press, 1989), 45.

13. John Sutton, *Psychic Pets* (Hillsboro, Ore.: Beyond Words Publishing, Inc., 1997), 73.

14. Nina Epton, *Cat Manners and Mysteries* (London, UK: Michael Joseph Limited, 1973), 38–39.

15. D. Scott Rogo, *Mind Beyond the Body: The Mystery of ESP Projection* (New York, N.Y.: Penguin Books, 1978), 176–178.

16. Richard Webster, *Astral Travel for Beginners* (St. Paul, Minn.: Llewellyn Publications, 1998).

17. Helmut Schmidt, "PK Experiments with Animals as Subjects," *Journal of Parapsychology* 34 (1970): 255–261.

18. Dr. Milton Kreutzer, quoted in *Your Pet's Secret Language* by Jhan Robbins (New York, N.Y.: Warner Books, Inc., 1975), 123.

19. John Malone, *The 125 Most Asked Questions About Cats (and the Answers)* (New York, N.Y.: William Morrow and Company, Inc., 1992), 88.

20. Jeane Dixon, *Do Cats Have ESP?* (New York, N.Y.: Aaron Publishing Group, 1998), 39–40. This experiment was also performed under laboratory conditions. A kitten would be placed in a T-shaped maze and an experimenter would will the cat to go either left or right to follow a predetermined sequence. As the results of this test were promising, the experiment was taken a step further. A bowl of food was placed at the end of one arm of the maze. An electric fan

was used to blow away any scent of the food. An experimenter again willed the kitten toward the food. Again, the results were well above the chance level. K. Osis and E. B. Foster, "A Test of ESP in Cats," *Journal of Parapsychology* 17 (1953): 168–186.

Chapter Three

1. Martyn Lewis, *Dogs in the News* (London, UK: Little, Brown and Company, Limited, 1992), 4. This was true when *Cats in the News* was published. However, since then, the number of dogs in Britain has declined, while the number of cats has increased. There are now more cats than dogs in Britain, although more households contain dogs than cats. This is because many homes contain two or more cats. The same trend has been apparent in the United States where there are now 59,000,000 cats and 53,000,000 dogs (Humane Society of America, Washington, D.C., 1996).

2. Elizabeth Marshall Thomas, *The Hidden Life of Dogs* (New York, N.Y.: The Houghton Mifflin Company, 1993), 3–4.

3. June Whitfield, *Dogs' Tales* (London, UK: Robson Books Limited, 1987), 113.

4. Paulette Cooper and Paul Noble, *277 Secrets Your Dog Wants You to Know*, 30.

5. Aaron Honori Katcher and Alan M. Beck, *New Perspectives on Our Lives with Companion Animals*, 351–359.

6. V. L. Voith, "Behaviors, Attitudes and Interactions of Families with Their Dogs," a paper presented at the Conferences on the Human-Animal Bond, Irvine, Calif., and Minneapolis, Minn., June 1983.

7. June Whitfield, *Dogs' Tales*, 21.

8. Ibid., 33.

9. Hal Ryder, *Pompeii Revealed* (Chicago, Ill.: The Renault Company, 1946), 134.

10. Napoleon Bonaparte, quoted in Joseph Wylder, *Psychic Pets* (New York, N.Y.: Stonehill Publishing Company, 1978), 71–72.

11. Yvonne Roberts, *Animal Heroes* (London, UK: Pelham Books, 1990), 4–5.
    If your dog has done something heroic, you should tell Ken-L Rations about it. Each year three to four hundred dogs are nominated for the Ken-L Rations Dog Hero of the Year award, and the winner receives a year's supply of Kibbles 'n Bits dog food and a silver-plated dog bowl. To receive their guidelines, send a stamped, addressed envelope to Ken-L Rations Dog Hero of the Year Award, P.O. Box 1370, Barrington, IL 60011.

12. Phyllis Galde, "I See By the Papers," *Fate Magazine* (St. Paul, Minn.: Llewellyn Publications, September 2000): 3.

13. The story of Gelert and Prince Llywellyn is one of the best-known folk tales in Wales. Sadly, it appears that the story may not be true, as Gelert's grave dates back only two hundred years. David Pritchard, the landlord of the Royal Goat Inn, wanted a promotional gimmick and "discovered" the "ancient" grave. Needless to say, business rapidly improved, and even today, thousands of tourists come to visit the grave every year.

14. Dr. Stanley Coren, *Why We Love the Dogs We Do*, 3–4.

15. Myrna M. Milani, *The Invisible Leash: A Better Way to Communicate with Your Dog* (New York, N.Y.: New American Library, 1985), 16.

16. Dr. Stanley Coren, *Why We Love the Dogs We Do*, 30–31.

17. June Whitfield, *Dogs' Tales*, 138.

18. Angela Patmore, *Your Obedient Servant: The Story of Man's Best Friend* (London, UK: Hutchinson and Company [Publishers] Limited, 1984), 95.

19. Dr. Rupert Sheldrake, *Dogs That Know When Their Owners Are Coming Home and Other Unexplained Powers of Animals* (London, UK: Hutchinson, 1999), 77.

20. J. Allen Boone, *Kinship with All Life* (New York, N.Y.: Harper & Row, Publishers, Inc., 1954), 35.

21. Dr. Rupert Sheldrake, *Dogs That Know When Their Owners Are Coming Home and Other Unexplained Powers of Animals*, 196–197.

22. Milan Ryzl, *Parapsychology: A Scientific Approach* (New York, N.Y.: Hawthorn Books, Inc., 1970), 141.

23. R. C. Finucane, *Appearances of the Dead: A Cultural History of Ghosts* (Buffalo, N.Y.: Prometheus Books, 1984), 145.

24. Dr. Stanley Coren, interview on *The Charlie Rose Show*, April 13, 1994.

25. Yvonne Roberts, *Animal Heroes*, 32.

26. Ibid, 69–70. Also Jilly Cooper, *Intelligent and Loyal* (London, UK: Eyre Methuen Limited, 1981), 204.

27. Martyn Lewis, *Dogs in the News*, 125–126.

28. Robert Morris, *Precognition in Laboratory Rats*. Quoted in *Prophecy in our Time* by Martin Ebon (New York, N.Y.: New American Library, Inc., 1968. Reprinted by Wilshire Book Company, Los Angeles, Calif., 1971), 174.

29. Jilly Cooper, *Mongrel Magic: A Celebration of the Mongrel* (London, UK: Eyre Methuen, Limited, 1981), 205.

30. *Proceedings*, volume XIII (New York, N.Y.: American Society for Psychical Research, 1919).

31. Nandor Fodor, *Encyclopaedia of Psychic Science* (New York, N.Y.: University Books, Inc., 1966), 4. (Originally published in 1934.)

32. Sheila Ostrander and Lynn Schroeder, *Psychic Discoveries Behind the Iron Curtain* (Englewood Cliffs, NJ: Prentice-Hall, Inc., 1970), 132–134.

33 Milan Ryzl, *Parapsychology: A Scientific Approach*, 152.

34. Joseph E. Wylder, *Psychic Pets* (New York, N.Y.: Stonehill Publishing Co., 1978), 131–132.

35. Alfred Douglas, *Extra Sensory Power: A Century of Psychical Research* (London, UK: Victor Gollancz Limited, 1976), 336–337.

36. The Russian experiment involved rabbits. The baby rabbits were placed on board a submarine and their mother was placed in a laboratory on shore. Electrodes were placed into her brain. When the submarine was deep down in the ocean, the baby rabbits were killed one by one. Each time a baby rabbit died, at the same moment a reaction occurred in the mother's brain. Sheila Ostrander and Lynn Schroeder, *Psychic Discoveries Behind the Iron Curtain* (Englewood Cliffs, N.J.: Prentice-Hall, Inc., 1970), 32–33.)

37. "See Spot See Blue," University of California at Santa Barbara, Calif., report in *Scientific American*, January 1990, 87–89.

38. Rolf Harris, *Tall Animal Tales* (London, UK: Headline Book Publishing, 2000), 227.

Chapter Four

1. Elwyn Hartley Edwards, *The Encyclopedia of the Horse* (New York, N.Y.: Dorling Kindersley Publishing, Inc., 1994), 70–71.

2. *The New Encyclopaedia Britannica*, Macropaedia, Volume 8 (Chicago, Ill.: Encyclopaedia Britannica, Inc., Fifteenth Edition, 1983), 1088.

3. Desmond Morris, *Horsewatching* (London, UK: Jonathan Cape Limited, 1988), 28.

4. Lawrence Scanlan, *Wild About Horses: Our Timeless Passion for the Horse* (New York, N.Y.: HarperCollins Publishers, Inc., 1998), 293.

5. Anna Sewell, *Black Beauty*. First published 1877. Available in many editions. My edition was published by William Collins Sons and Co. Limited, London, UK, 1953, 71.

6. Anthony Wootton, *Animal Folklore, Myth and Legend* (Poole, UK: Blandford Press, 1986), 68.

7. Lawrence Scanlan, *Wild About Horses: Our Timeless Passion for the Horse*, 295.

8 C. A. McCall, "A Review of Learning Behavior in Horses and its Applications in Horse Training," *Journal of Animal Science* 68 (1990): 75–81.

9. Henry Blake, *Talking with Horses* (New York, N.Y.: E. P. Dutton and Company, Inc., 1976.)

10. Terence Hines, *Pseudoscience and the Paranormal* (Buffalo, N.Y.: Prometheus Press, 1988), 83–84. In fact, because of their fear that Hans may have had genuine psychic ability, scientists missed out on an excellent opportunity to study the communicative skills of horses. This could—and

should—have led to a major study of communication between animals and humans.

11. Brian Inglis, *The Hidden Power* (London, UK: Jonathan Cape Limited, 1986), 194–195.

12. Nandor Fodor, *Encyclopaedia of Psychic Science*. Originally published in 1934. Republished by University Books, Inc., 1966, 4.

13. J. B. Rhine and L. E. Rhine, "An Investigation of a Mind-Reading Horse," *Journal of Abnormal Social Psychology* 23 (1929): 449–466. A follow-up report was included in volume 24 (1929): 287–292.

14. Jack Woodford, "Lady Was a Wonder," *Fate Magazine*, February 1963. Reprinted in *Psychic Pets and Spirit Animals* (St. Paul, Minn.: Llewellyn Publications, 1996), 13–23.

15. Dennis Bardens, *Psychic Animals* (New York, N.Y.: Henry Holt and Company, Inc., 1988), 119.

16. Phyllis Raybin Emert, *Mysteries of Bizarre Animals and Freaks of Nature* (New York, N.Y.: Tor Books, 1994), 26. This reporter remained skeptical, thinking that Mrs. Fonda had somehow coded the answer to Lady Wonder. Consequently, she asked Lady Wonder to tell her middle name. Lady Wonder immediately spelled out the correct answer, information she must have picked up clairvoyantly from the reporter.

17. Jack Woodford, "Lady was a Wonder," *Fate Magazine* (February 1963). Reprinted in *Psychic Pets and Spirit Animals* (Llewellyn Publications, St. Paul, Minn., 1996), 13–23.

18. Rolf Harris, *True Animal Tales* (London, UK: Random House, 1997), 133–134.

19. Case E. 423, *Proceedings of the Society for Psychical Research*, London, UK (Vol 53, Part 191, 1960).

20. H. Munro Fox, *The Personality of Animals* (London, UK: Penguin Books, 1940. Revised edition 1952), 48.

21. Harry Blake, *Talking with Horses: A Study of Communication Between Man and Horse* (London, UK: Souvenir Press, 1975), 131.

22. Ibid., 115–116.

Chapter Five

1. J. Allen Boone, *Kinship with All Life*, 145–149.

2. Anthony Wootton, *Animal Folklore, Myth and Legend*, 67–68.

3. Martin Ebon, *Prophecy in Our Time* (New York, N.Y.: The New American Library, Inc., 1968). My edition was published by Wilshire Book Company (North Hollywood, Calif., 1971), 173.

4. P. Duval and E. Montredon, "ESP Experiments with Mice," *Journal of Parapsychology* 32 (1968): 153–166.

5. W. J. Levy, L. A. Mayo, E. André, and A. McRae, "Repetition of the French Precognition Experiments with Mice," *Journal of Parapsychology* 35 (1971): 1–17.

6. John Randall, "Experiments to Detect a Psi Effect with Small Animals," *Journal of the Society for Physical Research* (1971): 46: 31–39.

7. *Into the Unknown* (Sydney, Australia: Reader's Digest Services Pty. Ltd., 1982), 242–244. Also Joseph E. Wylder, *Psychic Pets* (New York, N.Y.: Stonehill Publishing Company, 1978), 66.

8. D. Scott Rogo, "Do Animals Have ESP?" article in *Fate Magazine*, July 1986. Reprinted in *Psychic Pets and Spirit Animals* (St. Paul, Minn.: Llewellyn Publications, 1996), 35–36.

Chapter Six

1. Steven Drozdeck, Joseph Yeager, and Linda Sommer, *What They Don't Teach You in Sales 101: How Top Salespeople Recognize and Respond to Nonverbal Buying Signals* (New York, N.Y.: McGraw-Hill, Inc., 1991), xiv.

2. There are many sources for the story of James McKenzie. The most comprehensive is James McNeish, *The Mackenzie Affair* (Auckland, NZ: Hodder and Stoughton Limited, 1972).

3. Ann Walker, *Talk with the Animals* (Melbourne, Australia, Thomas Nelson Australia, 1983), 20.

4. Trillis Parker, *Horse's Talk: It Pays to Listen* (Las Vegas, Nev.: Parker Productions, Inc., revised edition 1989), 53.

5. J. Allen Boone, *Kinship with All Life*, 74–75 and 78–79.

6. Sheila Hocken, *Emma and I* (London, Sphere Books, 1978).

7. Tim Austin, *Dog Psychology* (Australia, Tim Austin, 1978).

8. Richard Webster, *Spirit Guides and Angel Guardians* (St. Paul, Minn.: Llewellyn Publications, 1998), 29–76.

Chapter Seven

1. Mrs. M. E. Dyett, "The Dog Ghost that Worked," *Dogs That Serve*, compiled by L. G. Cashmore (London, UK: George Ronald, 1960), 64–66.

2. William Bulstrode, *Tales of the British Raj* (London, UK: Curwen Publishing, 1898), 576.

3. Dorothy Bomar Bradley and Robert A. Bradley, M.D., *Psychic Phenomena* (New York, N.Y.: Warner Books, Inc., 1969), 76–77. Originally published by Parker Publishing Co., Inc., 1967.

4. Robert Campion Ennen, "Gerigio, the Phantom Dog of Turin," *Psychic Pets and Spirit Animals* (St. Paul, Minn.: Llewellyn Publications, 1996), 249–253. Originally published in *Fate Magazine*, November 1949.

5. Nina Epton, *Cat Manners and Mysteries*, 185–186.

6. *Proceedings of the Society for Psychical Research* (volume X), 127.

7. Mrs. Osborne Leonard, "Two Planes," *The International Psychic Gazette* (London, UK: The International Psychic Gazette Limited), April 1918.

8. What makes this story even more extraordinary is that Pekinese were not introduced to Britain until 1860, when four of these dogs were presented to Queen Victoria. However, by that time, the legend of the Daisy Dog was already hundreds of years old. Ruth L. Tongue's book *Forgotten Folk-Tales of the English Counties* (London, UK: Routledge and Kegan Paul, 1970), contains a number of accounts of people who have died after receiving a bite from this phantom dog.

9. Katharine Briggs, *A Dictionary of Fairies* (London, UK: Allen Lane Limited, 1976), 301.

10. Personal e-mails from Stefan Dardik, September 5–7, 2000.

11. Elliott O'Donnell, *Animal Ghosts* (London, UK: Farnell and Company, 1922), 78. Originally published 1913.

12. Leonard George, *Alternative Realities: The Paranormal, the Mystic and the Transcendent in Human Experience* (New York, N.Y.: Facts on File, Inc., 1995), 19.

Chapter Eight

1. Rolf Harris, Mark Leigh, and Mike Lepine, *True Animal Tales* (London, UK: Century Limited, 1996), 161.

2. Rolf Harris, Mark Leigh, and Mike Lepine, *True Animal Tales* (London, UK: Random House, 1997), 29–30.

3. John J. Kohut and Roland Sweet, *Strange Tails* (New York, N.Y.: Plume Books, 1999), 139.

4. Ibid., 139.

5. Ibid., 139.

6. Rolf Harris, *Tall Animal Stories* (London, UK: Headline Book Publishing, 2000), 59.

7. Sheila Burnford, *The Incredible Journey* (London, UK: Hodder and Stoughton Limited, 1961).

8. Rolf Harris, Mark Leigh, and Mike Lepine, *True Animal Tales*, 156.

9. Brian Inglis, *The Hidden Power*, 197.

10. J. B. Rhine and S. R. Feather, "The Study of Cases of 'Psi-Trailing' in Animals," *Journal of Parapsychology* 15 (1962): 1–22.

11. E. H. Herrick, "Homing Powers of the Cat," *Science Monthly* 14 (1922): 526–539.

12. Bastian Schmidt, "Vorläufiges Versuchsergebnis über das handliche Orienterungsproblem," *Zeitschrift für Hunderforschung* 2 (1932): 133–156. See also Bastian Schmidt, *Interviewing Animals* (London, UK: Allen and Unwin Limited, 1936).

13. Desmond Morris, *Catwatching* (London, UK: Jonathan Cape Limited, 1986), 94–95.

14. G. H. Lemish, *The Dogs of War: Canines in Combat* (Washington, D.C.: Brassey and Company, Inc., 1996), 220.

15. Milan Ryzl, *Parapsychology: A Scientific Approach*, 141.

16. Dr. J. B. Rhine, *New World of the Mind* (New York, N.Y.: William Sloane Associates, 1953), 178–179.

Chapter Nine

1. Diane Tennant, "The Horse Psychic," *The New Zealand Society of Dowsing and Radionics (Inc.) Journal* 24 (1, March 2001): 11. Originally published in *The American Dowser* (Summer, 2000).

2. *Species-Link: A Journal of Interspecies Communication* is published quarterly by Pegasus Publications, P.O. Box 1060, Point Reyes, CA 94956. (415) 663-1247.

Chapter Ten

1. Peter and Elizabeth Fenwick, *The Hidden Door* (London, UK: Headline Book Publishing, 1997), 156.

2. Ibid., 5.

3. *MIT News*, "Animals Have Complex Dreams, MIT Researcher Proves" (Cambridge, Mass: January 24, 2001.)

4. Hervey de Saint-Denys, *Dreams and How to Guide Them*, translated by N. Fry, edited and with an introduction by Morton Schatzman (London, UK: Duckworth and Company, 1982). Originally published in 1867.

5. Colin Wilson, *Beyond the Occult* (London, Guild Publishing, 1988), 154–155.

SUGGESTED READING

Adams, Janine. *You Can Talk To Your Animals.* Foster City, Calif.: IDG Books Worldwide, Inc., 2000.

Alexander, Charles. *Bobbie: A Great Collie of Oregon.* New York, N.Y.: Dodd Mead and Company, 1926.

Anderson, Allen and Linda. *Angel Animals: Exploring Our Spiritual Connection with Animals.* New York, N.Y.: Penguin Putnam, Inc., 1999.

Asbell, Bernard. *The Book of You.* New York, N.Y.: Fawcett Columbine, 1991.

Bardens, Dennis. *Psychic Animals.* New York, N.Y.: Henry Holt and Company, Inc., 1988.

Blake, Harry. *Talking with Horses: A Study of Communication Between Man and Horse.* London, UK: Souvenir Press, 1975. New York, N.Y.: E. P. Dutton and Company, Inc., 1976. Republished by Trafalgar Square Publishing, Vermont, 1990.

———. *Horse Sense.* North Pomfret, Vt.: Trafalgar Square Publishing, 1994.

Boone, J. Allen. *Kinship with All Life.* New York, N.Y.: Harper & Row, 1954.

Bright, Michael. *The Dolittle Obsession.* London, UK: Robson Books Limited, 1990.

Budiansky, Stephen. *The Nature of Horses: Exploring Equine Evolution, Intelligence and Behavior.* New York, N.Y.: The Free Press, 1997.

Burton, Maurice. *The Sixth Sense of Animals.* London, UK: J. M. Dent & Sons Limited, 1973.

Burton, Robert. *Animal Senses.* Newton Abbott, UK: David and Charles (Publishers) Limited, 1970.

Caras, Roger A. *A Dog Is Listening.* New York, N.Y.: Summit Books, 1992.

Cooper, Jilly. *Mongrel Magic: A Celebration of the Mongrel.* London, UK: Eyre Methuen Ltd., 1981.

———. *Intelligent and Loyal.* London, UK: Eyre Methuen Limited, 1981.

Cooper, Paulette, and Paul Noble. *277 Secrets Your Dog Wants You to Know.* Berkeley, Calif.: Ten Speed Press, 1995.

Coren, Dr. Stanley. *The Intelligence of Dogs: Canine Consciousness and Capabilities.* New York, N.Y.: The Free Press/ Macmillan Publishing, 1994.

———. *Why We Love The Dogs We Do.* New York, N.Y.: The Free Press, 1998.

Dale-Green, Patricia. *Cult of the Cat.* New York, N.Y.: Houghton Mifflin Company, 1963.

Dixon, Jeane. *Do Cats Have ESP?* New York, N.Y.: Aaron Publishing Group, 1998.

Dodman, Dr. Nicholas. *The Cat Who Cried for Help.* New York, N.Y.: Bantam Books, 1997.

Downer, John. *Supersense: Perception in the Animal World.* New York, N.Y.: Henry Holt and Company, Inc., 1989.

Durov, Vladimir. *Training of Animals.* London, UK: George Routledge and Sons, 1937.

Ebon, Martin. *Prophecy in Our Time.* New York, N.Y.: The New American Library, Inc., 1968.

Eckstein, Warren, with Fay Eckstein. *How to Get Your Cat to Do What You Want.* New York, N.Y.: Villard Books, 1991.

Edwards, Elwyn Hartley. *The Ultimate Horse Book.* London, UK: Dorling Kindersley Limited, 1991.

Emert, Phyllis Raybin. *Mysteries of Bizarre Animals and Freaks of Nature.* New York, N.Y.: Tor Books, 1994.

Epton, Nina. *Cat Manners and Mysteries.* London, UK: Michael Joseph Ltd., 1973.

Evans, George Ewart. *Horse Power and Magic.* London, UK: Faber and Faber Limited, 1979.

Fate Magazine. *Psychic Pets and Spirit Animals.* St. Paul, Minn.: Llewellyn Publications, 1996.

Fitzpatrick, Sonya, with Patricia Burkhart Smith. *What the Animals Tell Me.* New York, N.Y.: Hyperion Books, 1997.

Fogle, Dr. Bruce. *The Dog's Mind: Understanding Your Dog's Behavior.* New York, N.Y.: Howell Book House, 1990.

Freedman, Russell, and James E. Morriss. *Animal Instincts.* New York, N.Y.: Holiday House, Inc., 1970.

Gallico, Paul. *The Silent Miaow.* New York, N.Y.: Crown Publishers, Inc., 1964.

Gooch, Stan. *The Secret Life of Humans.* London, UK: J. M. Dent & Sons Limited, 1981.

Gordon, Stuart. *The Paranormal: An Illustrated Encyclopedia.* London, UK: Headline Book Publishing, 1992.

Gould, James L., and Carol Grant Gould. *The Animal Mind.* New York, N.Y.: Scientific American Library, 1994.

Harris, Rolf. *Tall Animal Stories.* London, UK: Headline Book Publishing, 2000.

Hart, Stephen. *The Language of Animals.* New York, N.Y.: Henry Holt and Company, Inc., 1996.

Haynes, Renee. *The Seeing Eye, The Seeing I: Perception, Sensory and Extra-Sensory.* London, UK: Hutchinson and Co. (Publishers) Limited, 1976.

Hearne, Vicki. *Adam's Task: Calling Animals by Name.* London, UK: William Heinemann Limited, 1987.

Hodson, Geoffrey. *Authentic Stories of Intelligence in Animals.* Auckland, NZ: The Council of Combined Animal Welfare Organisation of New Zealand, n.d.

Holland, Barbara. *The Name of the Cat.* New York, N.Y.: Dodd, Mead and Company, 1988.

Howey, M. Oldfield. *The Cat in Magic, Mythology and Religion.* New York, N.Y.: Crescent Books, 1989. (Originally published as *The Cat in the Mysteries of Religion and Magic* by Rider and Company, London, n.d.)

"Into the Unknown." Sydney, Australia: Reader's Digest Services Pty. Limited, 1982.

Jenkins, Sid. *Animals Have More Sense.* London, UK: William Collins Sons and Company Limited, 1987.

Kindermann, Henny. *Lola: Or the Thought and Speech of Animals.* (No publisher listed), 1922.

Lorenz, Konrad. *Man Meets Dog.* London, UK: Penguin Books, 1953.

Loxton, Howard. *99 Lives: Cats in History, Legend and Literature.* San Francisco, Calif.: Chronicle Books, 1998.

Lydecker, Beatrice. *What the Animals Tell Me.* New York, N.Y.: Harper & Row, 1977.

Maeterlinck, Morris. *The Unknown Guest.* London, UK: Methuen and Company Limited, 1914. New York, N.Y.: Dodd, Mead, and Company, 1914.

Meyer, Judy. *The Animal Connection.* New York, N.Y.: Penguin Putnam, Inc., 2000.

Milani, Myrna M. *The Invisible Leash: A Better Way to Communicate with Your Dog.* New York, N.Y.: New American Library, 1985.

Morris, Desmond. *Catwatching.* London, UK: Jonathan Cape Limited, 1986.

————. *Horsewatching.* London, UK: Jonathan Cape Limited, 1988.

Myers, Arthur. *Communicating with Animals.* Chicago, IL: Contemporary Books, 1997. (This book also includes a listing of animal communicators in the United States and Canada.)

Nollman, Jim. *Animal Dreaming.* New York, N.Y.: Bantam Books, 1987.

Parker, Steve. *How Do We Know Animals Can Think?* Austin, Tex.: Raintree Steck-Vaughn Publishers, 1995.

Patmore, Angela. *Your Obedient Servant: The Story of Man's Best Friend.* London, UK: Hutchinson and Company (Publishers) Limited, 1984.

Redgrove, Peter. *The Black Goddess and the Sixth Sense.* London, UK: Bloomsbury Publishing Limited, 1987.

Rhine, J. B. *New World of the Mind.* New York, N.Y.: William Sloane Associates, 1953.

Rhine, J. B., and J. G. Pratt. *Parapsychology: Frontier Science of the Mind.* Springfield, Ill.: Charles C. Thomas, 1957. Revised edition 1962.

Roberts, Monty. *The Man Who Listens to Horses.* New York, N.Y.: Random House, Inc., 1997.

Roberts, Yvonne. *Animal Heroes.* London, UK: Pelham Books, 1990.

Rowdon, Maurice. *The Talking Dogs.* London, UK: Macmillan and Company Limited, 1978.

Sales, Gillian, and David Pye. *Ultrasonic Communication by Animals.* London, UK: Chapman and Hall Limited, 1974.

Scanlan, Lawrence. *Wild About Horses: Our Timeless Passion for the Horse.* New York, N.Y.: HarperCollins Publishers, Inc., 1998.

Schul, Bill. *The Psychic Power of Animals.* London, UK: Coronet Books/Hodder & Stoughton Limited, 1978.

Sheldrake, Rupert. *Dogs That Know When Their Owners Are Coming Home and Other Unexplained Powers of Animals.* London, UK: Hutchinson, 1999.

Smith, Penelope. *Animal Talk.* Hillsboro, Ore.: Beyond Words Publishing, INC., 1999. (Originally published by Pegasus Publications in 1982.)

———. *Animals . . . Our Return to Wholeness.* Point Reyes, Calif.: Pegasus Publications, 1993.

Sparks, John. *The Discovery of Animal Behaviour.* London, UK: William Collins Sons and Company Limited, 1982.

Steiger, Brad. *Man and Dog.* New York, N.Y.: Donald I. Fine, Inc., 1995.

Sutton, John. *Psychic Pets.* Hillsboro, Ore.: Beyond Words Publishing, Inc., 1997.

Thomas, Elizabeth Marshall. *The Hidden Life of Dogs.* New York, N.Y.: The Houghton Mifflin Company, 1993.

Thomas, Warren D., and Daniel Kaufman. *Elephant Midwives, Parrot Duets and Other Intriguing Facts About the Animal Kingdom.* London, UK: Robson Books Limited, 1991.

Tributsch, Helmut. *When the Snakes Awake: Animals and Earthquake Prediction.* Cambridge, Mass.: The MIT Press,

1982. (Originally published as *Wenn die Schlangen Erwachen* by Deitsche Verlags-Anstalt GmbH, Stuttgart, Germany, 1978.)

Walker, Ann. *Talk with the Animals.* Melbourne, Australia: Thomas Nelson, 1983.

Whitfield, June. *Dogs' Tales.* London, UK: Robson Books Limited, 1987.

Whittemore, Hank, and Caroline Hebard. *So That Others May Live: Caroline Hebard and her Search-and-Rescue Dogs.* New York, N.Y.: Bantam Books, 1995.

Williams, Rev. Charles. *Dogs and Their Ways.* London, UK: George Routledge and Company, 1865.

Woodhouse, Barbara. *Talking to Animals.* London, UK: Fontana Books, 1974.

———. *Almost Human.* London, UK: Penguin Books, 1981.

Wootton, Anthony. *Animal Folklore, Myth and Legend.* Poole, UK: Blandford Press, 1986.

Wylder, Joseph. *Psychic Pets.* New York, N.Y.: Stonehill Publishing Company, 1978.

Zeuner, Frederick E. *A History of Domesticated Animals.* New York, N.Y.: Harper & Row, 1963.

Index

Adolphe, xiii–xiv

Airedale, 48, 50

Alexander, Charles, 143

alfalfa, 7

Alsatian, 55

American Society for
  Psychical Research, 32

angel guardians, 112, 114,
  116, 123, 158

animal communicator,
  111–112, 114, 149, 151,
  166–167

animal psychics, 164,
  166

ants, 4, 11

apparitions, 121, 136–138

astral travel, 27

Austin, Tim, 107

Babieca, 68

Baker, Richard St. Barbe, xiii

Barghest, 132

basset hound, 50

Bastet, 20–21

Bekhterov, Vladimir M.,
  55–56

Berkland, Jim, 9–10

Berto, 75

Bessant, Malcolm, 170

birds and singing, 6

birds of prey, 4

Black Bear, 76–77

Blake, Henry, 74

bloodhound, 3

Bobbie, 143

body language
    and crossed hands, 100
    and tails, 25, 72, 73

Bonaparte, Napoleon, 39

Boone, J. Allen, 45, 88, 104

border collie, 41

Borley Rectory, 121

boxer, 58–59

Bradley, Robert, 122

Brown, James, 51

Bruce, xiv, 24–25, 62, 65, 102, 105, 124–125, 147

bull terrier, 143

bumblebees, 7

Burdett-Coutts, Baroness, 40

Burnford, Sheila, 143

Cadoret, Remi, 57–58

Caligula, 68

Chambers, Sir William, 40

Charles I, 23

Charles II, 37

Chaucer, Geoffrey, 39

Chauvin, R., 89

Chesapeake Bay, 6

Chester, 142

Chihuahua, 122

China, 23, 36, 130

Ching, 126

chow, 43

Chris the Wonder Dog, 57

Churchill, Winston, 23

clairvoyance, 8, 12, 64, 76

Clementine, 145

Clever Hans, 74–76

Clyde, xii, 12, 29, 151

collie, 41, 46, 143

contacting a departed pet, 137, 139

Cooper, Mark, 39

Coren, Dr. Stanley, x, 49

Cork Beg, 84

Crowther, A. H., 9

Custer, General George Armstrong, 37

Cyprus, 15

Daisy, 130, 141

Daisy Dog, 130

Dardik, Stefan, 133

de Lenclos, Ninon, 37

Dement, William, 170

D'Hervey de Saint-Denys, Marquis, 173

Don Bosco, 122–123

Dozmary Pool, 130

dreams, 79–80, 93, 120, 155, 169–180

duck, 88

Duke University, 27, 32, 57, 64, 77, 145

Dumas, Alexandre, xii

Durov, Vladimir, 55–56

Duval, Pierre, 88

earthquakes, animal behavior before, 10–11, 18, 19, 69–70

Edney, Andrew, 46

Eeden, Frederik Van, 173

Egypt, 15, 21

Egyptians, 18, 20–21, 169

El Cid, 67–68

Elberfeld, 74–76

electric eel, 2

electric ray, 2

elephants, 2, 69

Elizabeth I, 37, 130

Emma, 106–107

Epton, Nina, 123

ESP, 58

Esser, Aristed, 58

evolution, 1

eyesight, 4

cat eyesight, 16

dog eyesight, 1

horse eyesight, 69

Faith, 19

fish, 6, 8, 11, 90, 165

Fonda, Claudia, 77–80

Foundation for Research on the Nature of Man, 52

Freud, Sigmund, 43, 169

Friesian, 141

frogs, 3, 87, 91

geese, 88

Gelert, 41–42

Gerigio, 122–123

German shepherd, 24, 39, 45, 49, 51

ghosts, 18, 47, 119–139, 155

golden Labrador, 8

Grant, Sir Robert, 121

Greyfriar's Bobby, 40

guardian angel, 114, 116, 158

guide dogs, 37, 106–107

Gundo, 51–52

Hachiko, 41

Hakelnberg, 135

Hancock, Geoff, 143

hearing range, 2

    cat hearing, 2, 17

    dog hearing, 2

    horse hearing, 69

Hector, 12–13

Herne the Hunter, 136

Herrick, F. H., 145

Hocken, Sheila, 106

honeybees, 6, 7–8

Hormus, 21

Howard, Lady, 135

hydrophones, 6

Incitatus, 68

Inka, 108–109

Innocent VII, Pope, 22

instinct, 6–7, 107

Institut de Psychologie
    Zoologique, 96

Institute for Parapsychology,
    89

interspecies communication,
    31, 94, 167

invisible friends, 125

Isis, 21

Italian greyhound, 37

Japanese bobtail, 28

Jo-Fi, 43

Johnson, Lyndon B., 171

Jones, Mrs. Gordon, 125–126

Jung, Carl, 169

Kearns, Doris, 171

Ken-L Rations, 39

Khai-hwang, Emperor, 23

Killy, 101–102

Kimball, Fred, 72

Kindermann, Henny, 54

Kleitman, Nathaniel, 170

Krall, Karl, 74–76

Labrador retriever, 43

Lady Wonder, 77–80

le Brun, Alaine, 15

Leonard, Mrs. Gladys
    Osborne, 126–127

Leontovitch, Alexander,
    55

Lewis, Martyn, 35

Lily, 50

Llywellyn, Prince, 41–42

Lola, 53–54

lost pets, 141, 148–149, 151, 153

Louie, Kenway, 173

lucid dreams, 173–180

Lucky, 26

Mackall, Harry, 132

Mackenzie, William, 53, 96

Maeterlinck, Maurice, 76

magnetic field, 5, 11, 19

magnetite, 5

Maimonides Dream Laboratory, 170

Mannheim, 53–54

Margate, 23

Margot, 48, 150

Mars, 55–56

Mary, Queen of Scots, 37

mastiff, 37

mathematics and pets, 53–54, 74, 76

Matson, Danny, 77

Max, 145

McKenzie, James, 95–96

M'Comisky, J. G., ix

Meneki-neko, 28

Messina, 10, 18

Meyer, J., 89

mice, 5, 15, 18, 88–89, 125

Mickey, 126–127

Middle Ages, 22

Mika, 108–109

Mischka, 119–120, 122

Moeckel, Paula, 53–54

monarch butterflies, 5

Montgomery, William, 22

Montredon, Evelyn, 88

Morris, Robert, 52, 90

Mugford, R. A., ix

Muhamed, 75–76

Mysouff, xii

Native Americans, ix

Northern, Bill, 167

numbfish, 1–2

Odin, 136

Osis, Dr. Karlis, 32

palomino, 79

parrot, 96–97

Pekinese, 126, 130–131

Peritas, 37

Perkins, Hugh, 89

Persia, 21

pet ownership, benefits of, ix–x, 36

pet saviors, 152–153

Peter the Great, 37

pets as therapy animals, x

Pfungst, Otto, 75

Phoenicia, 79–80

pigeon, 90

Pikki, 56

pit viper, 4

Pliny the Elder, 1, 10

Plutarch, 88

Pompeii, 38

precognition, 11, 46, 53, 70, 78–79, 170–171

Prince, 51

psychic awareness exercise, 161–162

psychokinesis, 27

purring, 17–18, 25

Ra, 21

rabbit, 9, 97–98

Rameses the Great, 36

Randall, John, 89

Raton, 37–38

rats, 9–10, 15, 18, 20, 23, 89, 173

relaxation exercise, 158–160

REM, 170, 173, 177

Rhine, Dr. J. B., 9, 27, 57, 89, 144

Rhine, Dr. Louisa, 170

Richardson, William, 146–147

Rogers, Roy, 79

Rolf, 53–54

Roosevelt, President, 78

Rover, 120–122

Ryzl, Dr. Milan, 46, 147

salmon, 4

Sam, 142

Scanlen, Winslow, 120

Schmidt, Bastian, 145, 148

Schmidt, Helmut, 27

Schwarzl, Josef, 8

Sebastian, 165

Senbi, 35

Sewell, Anna, 70

Sheldrake, Dr. Rupert, xv–xvi, 44

Shih Tzu, 49

shuck, 132

Siamese, 24–25, 110, 123, 143, 181

Skye terrier, 37

smell, sense of, 3–4, 17, 43–44, 69, 146

    cat sense of smell, 17

    dog sense of smell, 1, 3, 43

    horse sense of smell, 69

Snow, Linda, 164

Sophie, 26

Speer, Rhonda, 151

Spencer, William Robert, 42

Spot, 141–142

springer spaniel, 44

Steiner, Johann, 51

Stone Carr, 35

Strongheart, 45

Stumpf, Professor C., 75

Sugar, 144

Swindon, H. G., 127

telepathy, 12, 26, 29, 32, 44, 56, 61, 65, 80, 116

Thorssen, Linda, 111, 117

Tibbar, 97–98

Ting, 24, 110–111

Toby, 8

Tompkins, Jed, 47

Tony, 143–144

Trash, 132

Tregeagle, Jan, 130

Trigger, 79

Troubles, 146

Truman, Harry, 78

Ueno, Dr. Eisaburo, 41

Vesuvius, 38

Weir, Major, 136

whales, 5, 69

Whisky, 143

William, 12, 22, 40, 42, 44–45, 53, 146–147, 170

Williams, 42

Wilson, Matthew, 172

Winston, 23, 43

witches, 22

wolves, 8, 38, 148

Wootton, Anthony, 71

wraith, 137–139

Wright, Wilbur, 180

Zarif, 75

Zener cards, 57

Zoopsychological
    Laboratory, 56

Zooveterinary Institute, 56

Zorro, 39

☾ REACH FOR THE MOON

Llewellyn publishes hundreds of books on your favorite subjects!
To get these exciting books, including the ones on the following pages,
check your local bookstore or order them directly from Llewellyn.

Order by Phone
- Call toll-free within the U.S. and Canada, 1-877-NEW-WRLD
- In Minnesota, call (651) 291-1970
- We accept VISA, MasterCard, and American Express

Order by Mail
- Send the full price of your order (MN residents add 7% sales tax)
  in U.S. funds, plus postage & handling to:
  Llewellyn Worldwide
  P.O. Box 64383, Dept. 0-7387-0193-9
  St. Paul, MN 55164–0383, U.S.A.

Postage & Handling
- **Standard** (U.S., Mexico, & Canada)

If your order is:

$20.00 or under, add $5.00

$20.01–$100.00, add $6.00

Over $100, shipping is free

(Continental U.S. orders ship UPS. AK, HI, PR, & P.O. Boxes ship USPS 1st class. Mex. & Can. ship PMB.)

- **Second Day Air** (Continental U.S. only): $10.00 for one book + $1.00
  per each additional book
- **Express** (AK, HI, & PR only) [Not available for P.O. Box delivery. For
  street address delivery only.]: $15.00 for one book + $1.00 per each
  additional book
- **International Surface Mail:** Add $1.00 per item
- **International Airmail:** Books—Add the retail price of each item;
  Non-book items—Add $5.00 per item

Please allow 4–6 weeks for delivery on all orders.
Postage and handling rates subject to change.

Discounts
We offer a 20% discount to group leaders or agents. You must
order a minimum of 5 copies of the same book to get our
special quantity price.

FREE CATALOG
Get a free copy of our color catalog, *New Worlds of
Mind and Spirit.* Subscribe for just $10.00 in the Unit-
ed States and Canada ($30.00 overseas, airmail).

Visit our website at www.llewellyn.com for more information.

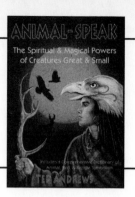

Animal-Speak

The Spiritual & Magical Powers
of Creatures Great & Small

TED ANDREWS

The animal world has much to teach us. Some are experts at survival and adaptation, some never get cancer, some embody strength and courage, while others exude playfulness. Animals remind us of the potential we can unfold, but before we can learn from them, we must first be able to speak with them.

In this book, myth and fact are combined in a manner that will teach you how to speak and understand the language of the animals in your life. *Animal-Speak* helps you meet and work with animals as totems and spirits—by learning the language of their behaviors within the physical world. It provides techniques for reading signs and omens in nature so you can open to higher perceptions and even prophecy. It reveals the hidden, mythical, and realistic roles of 45 animals, 60 birds, 8 insects, and 6 reptiles.

Animals will become a part of you, revealing to you the majesty and divine in all life. They will restore your childlike wonder of the world and strengthen your belief in magic, dreams, and possibilities.

0-87542-028-1

400 pp., 7 x 10, illus., photos $19.95

To order, call 1-877-NEW-WRLD
Prices subject to change without notice

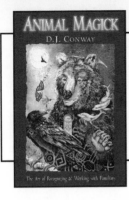

Animal Magick

The Art of Recognizing & Working with Familiars

D. J. CONWAY

The use of animal familiars began long before the Middle Ages in Europe. It can be traced to ancient Egypt and beyond. To most people, a familiar is a witch's companion, a small animal that helps the witch perform magick, but you don't have to be a witch to have a familiar. In fact you don't even have to believe in familiars to have one. You may already have a physical familiar living in your home in the guise of a pet. Or you may have an astral-bodied familiar if you are intensely drawn to a particular creature that is impossible to have in the physical. There are definite advantages to befriending a familiar. They make excellent companions, even if they are astral creatures. If you work magick, the familiar can aid by augmenting your power. Familiars can warn you of danger, and they are good healers.

Most books on animal magick are written from the viewpoint of the Native American. This book takes you into the exciting field of animal familiars from the European Pagan viewpoint. It gives practical meditations, rituals, and power chants for enticing, befriending, understanding, and using the magick of familiars.

1-56718-168-6

256 pp., 6 x 9 $13.95

To order, call 1-877-NEW-WRLD
Prices subject to change without notice

Psychic Pets & Spirit Animals

FATE Magazine
Editorial Staff

True stories from the files of FATE magazine!

In spite of all our scientific knowledge about animals, important questions remain about the nature of animal intelligence. Now, a large body of personal testimony compels us to raise still deeper questions. Are some animals, like some people, psychic? If human beings survive death, do animals? Do bonds exist between people and animals that are beyond our ability to comprehend?

Psychic Pets & Spirit Animals is a varied collection from the past fifty years of the real-life experiences of ordinary people with creatures great and small. You will encounter psychic pets, ghost animals, animal omens, extraordinary human-animal bonds, pet survival after death, phantom protectors, and the weird creatures of cryptozoology. Dogs, cats, birds, horses, wolves, grizzly bears—even insects—are the heroes of shockingly true reports that illustrate just how little we know about the animals we think we know best.

The true stories in *Psychic Pets & Spirit Animals* suggest that animals are, in many ways, more like us than we think— and that they, too, can step into the strange and unknowable realm of the paranormal, where all things are possible.

1-56718-299-2

272 pp., mass market $4.99

Spirit Guides & Angel Guardians

Contact Your Invisible Helpers

RICHARD WEBSTER

They come to our aid when we least expect it, and they disappear as soon as their work is done. Invisible helpers are available to all of us; in fact, we all regularly receive messages from our guardian angels and spirit guides but usually fail to recognize them. This book will help you to realize when this occurs. And when you carry out the exercises provided, you will be able to communicate freely with both your guardian angels and spirit guides.

You will see your spiritual and personal growth take a huge leap forward as soon as you welcome your angels and guides into your life. This book contains numerous case studies that show how angels have touched the lives of others, just like yourself. Experience more fun, happiness, and fulfillment than ever before. Other people will also notice the difference as you become calmer, more relaxed, and more loving than ever before.

1-56718-795-1

368 pp., 5³⁄₁₆ x 8 $9.95

Palm Reading for Beginners

Find the Future in the Palm of Your Hand

Richard Webster

Announce in any gathering that you read palms and you will be flocked by people thrilled to show you their hands. When you are have finished *Palm Reading for Beginners*, you will be able to look at anyone's palm (including your own) and confidently and effectively tell them about their personality, love life, hidden talents, career options, prosperity, and health.

Palmistry is possibly the oldest of the occult sciences, with basic principles that have not changed in 2,600 years. This step-by-step guide clearly explains the basics, as well as advanced research conducted in the past few years on such subjects as dermatoglyphics.

Now you can learn to read palms even if you have no prior knowledge of the subject.

1-56718-791-9
264 pp., 5³⁄₁₆ x 8, illus. $9.95

Write Your Own Magic
The Hidden Power in Your Words

RICHARD WEBSTER

Write your innermost dreams
and watch them come true!

This book will show you how to use the incredible power of words to create the life that you have always dreamed about. We all have desires, hopes and wishes. Sadly, many people think theirs are unrealistic or unattainable. *Write Your Own Magic* shows you how to harness these thoughts by putting them to paper.

Once a dream is captured in writing it becomes a goal, and your subconscious mind will find ways to make it happen. From getting a date for Saturday night to discovering your purpose in life, you can achieve your goals, both small and large. You will also learn how to speed up the entire process by making a ceremony out of telling the universe what it is you want. With the simple instructions in this book, you can send your energies out into the world and magnetize all that is happiness, success, and fulfillment to you.

0-7387-0001-0
312 pp., 5³⁄₁₆ x 8 $9.95

To order, call 1-877-NEW-WRLD
Prices subject to change without notice

Feng Shui for Beginners

Successful Living by Design

RICHARD WEBSTER

Not advancing fast enough in your career? Maybe your desk is located in a "negative position." Wish you had a more peaceful family life? Hang a mirror in your dining room and watch what happens. Is money flowing out of your life rather than into it? You may want to look to the construction of your staircase!

For thousands of years, the ancient art of feng shui has helped people harness universal forces and lead lives rich in good health, wealth, and happiness. The basic techniques in *Feng Shui for Beginners* are very simple, and you can put them into place immediately in your home and work environments. Gain peace of mind, a quiet confidence, and turn adversity to your advantage with feng shui remedies.

1-56718-803-6

240 pp., 5¼ x 8, photos, diagrams $12.95